South University Library
Richmond Campus
2151 Old Brick Road
Glen Allen, Va 23060

D1787100

FEB 1 5 2012

Female Offenders and Risk Assessment
Hidden in Plain Sight

Janet T. Davidson

LFB Scholarly Publishing LLC
El Paso 2009

Copyright © 2009 by LFB Scholarly Publishing LLC

All rights reserved.

Library of Congress Cataloging-in-Publication Data

Davidson, Janet (Janet T.)
 Female offenders and risk assessment: hidden in plain sight / Janet T. Davidson.
   p. cm. -- (Criminal justice: recent scholarship)
 Includes bibliographical references and index.
 ISBN 978-1-59332-377-6 (hbk. : alk. paper)
 1. Female offenders--Rehabilitation. 2. Recidivism. 3. Corrections--United States. I. Title.
 HV6046.D28 2009
 364.3--dc22
                                    2009035636

ISBN 978-1-59332-377-6

Printed on acid-free 250-year-life paper.

Manufactured in the United States of America.

Table of Contents

Table of Contents v

List of Tables vii

List of Figures ix

Acknowledgements xi

Chapter 1: Female Offenders and Management Responses 1
Hidden in Plain Sight 1
How Gender Matters 3
Challenging the Past: Gender Matters & Feminist Epistemology 5
Misunderstanding to 'Benign Neglect' 7
Correctional Growth and Risk/Need Assessment Instruments 12
Conclusion 14

Chapter 2: A Brief History of Risk Management & Gender 17
Correctional Growth and the Use of Actuarial Risk/Need Instruments ... 17
Calculating Risk – A General Overview 19
The Evolution of Actuarial Risk/Need Instruments in Criminal Justice .. 24
Gender Matters in the Usage of Third Generation Risk/Need
Instruments 28
Current Gender-Relevant LSI-R & Risk/Need Instrument Research 36
Implications of the LSI-R for the Female Offender 43
Conclusion 46

Chapter 3: Making Gender Count:
Measuring the Impact of Gender in Risk & Need Instruments 49
Introduction 49
Counting Within a Feminist Framework 50
Gendered Risk & Need Research: Gaining Momentum 53
Framework for the Current Study 55
Conclusion 71

Chapter 4: 'Counting' Out of Context 73
Counting Differences in Risks and Needs 73
Making it in the Community: Recidivism Rates 75
LSI-R Domain and Factor Differences 76
Correlation with Outcome 80
Survival Analyses 84
Kaplan-Meier Analyses of LSI-R Risk Categories and Domains,
by Gender 94
Over- and Under-Classification by Gender 106
Conclusion 108

Chapter 5: 'Counting' in Context – Exploring Risk Through a Gendered Lens 113
Introduction: Risk through a Gendered Lens 113
Offender Views on Categories Related to LSI-R Domains 115
What's Left Out of the LSI-R –
Histories of Victimization, Health Problems, and Other 143
Conclusion 151

Chapter 6: Re-Considering Female Offenders – Context Matters 157
Introduction: Gender Matters 157
Cause, Correlation, and Context in Risk/Need Assessments 163
Moving Forward with Risk/Need Instruments 169
Future Development and Research 171

References 179

Index 193

List of Tables

3.1	Quantitative Sample Description: Total, Male, and Female Sample	58
3.2	Qualitative Sample Description: Total, Male, and Female Sample	69
4.1	Overall Recidivism Rates by Gender (Percents)	75
4.2	Overall Recidivism Rates by Gender and by Agency (Percents)	75
4.3	Overall LSI-R Score by Gender	76
4.4	LSI-R Domain and Factor Mean Comparisons by Gender	78
4.5	Bivariate Correlations with Recidivism for LSI-R Total Score and Domains for the Entire Sample and Male and Female Only Samples	80
4.6	Comparison of Top Five Correlates of Recidivism for Men and Women	81
4.7	Cox Regression Model 1: LSI-R Risk Levels for Total Sample and Male and Female Only Samples	85
4.8	Cox Regression Model 2: LSI-R Domain Categories	86
4.9	Cox Regression Model 3: LSI-R Domains and Ethnicity	91
4.10	Cox Regression Model 4: LSI-R Domains and Agency	92
4.11	Cox Regression Model 5: LSI-R Domains and Type of Crime	93

List of Figures

4.1	Survival Curve – Time to Recidivism, All Offenders	94
4.2	Time to Recidivism, by Gender and Agency	95
4.3	Time to Recidivism, by Classification Score & Gender	96
4.4	Time to Recidivism, by Criminal History Score & Gender	97
4.5	Time to Recidivism, by Education and Employment Score & Gender	98
4.6	Time to Recidivism, by Financial Score & Gender	99
4.7	Time to Recidivism, by Family and Marital Score & Gender	100
4.8	Time to Recidivism, by Accommodation Score & Gender	101
4.9	Time to Recidivism, by Leisure and Recreation Score & Gender	102
4.10	Time to Recidivism, by Companions Score and by Gender	103
4.11	Time to Recidivism, by Alcohol and Drug Score & Gender	104
4.12	Time to Recidivism, by Emotional and Personal Score & Gender	105
4.13	Time to Recidivism, by Attitudes and Orientation Score & Gender	106
4.14	Comparison of Gender by Classification Level (Percents)	107
4.15	Comparison of Recidivism Rates by Gender by Classification Level (Percents)	108

ACKNOWLEDGEMENTS

I am greatly indebted to Meda Chesney-Lind, who introduced me to the world of the female offender. Her passionate work in the field of feminist criminology is unmatched and her desire to do better for girls and women who are involved in the criminal justice system is contagious. Appreciation also goes to others who helped in various earlier parts of this work, including Robert Perkinson, David T. Johnson, Katherine Irwin, and Richard Baldoz.

Gene Kassebaum also requires special mention. Although Gene gave me my first real opportunity to 'get my hands dirty' in the criminal justice system, his biggest contribution came to me in casual conversation, namely in his advice to simply get it done.

I have been fortunate to be able to work with some very intelligent and knowledgeable individuals in the field of corrections in Hawai`i. Specifically, Cheryl Marlow, Ron Hajime, Kathy Shimata, Tommy Johnson, and Max Otani helped in various aspects of this work. Verdine Kong with the MEO project in Maui continues to support reentry for offenders in Maui and contributed to this project in a significant manner. Lorraine Robinson and Kat Brady both continue to inspire important work around female offenders and corrections generally.

I have received unprecedented support from my colleagues at Chaminade University of Honolulu. I am also fortunate to have many good friends who simply let me vent about this process. Specifically, Nancy Ralston and Ani Pang allow for the greatest moments of much needed laughter through difficult moments. Others have also had an immense impact on me personally and professionally, namely Paul Perrone, Nancy Marker, Lisa Pasko, Marilyn Brown, Christopher Bondy, RaeDeen Karasuda, Terri Hurst, and Meiko Arai. Thank you all for good advice and friendship throughout the years.

A special thanks must also be extended to all of the women and men who spent time with me, allowing me to ask them deeply personal questions about their past, present and future. This work would simply not have been possible without them.

CHAPTER 1

Female Offenders and Management Responses

Man is defined as a human being and woman as a female, whenever she behaves as a human being she is said to imitate the male.
-- Simone de Beauvoir

Hidden In Plain Sight

Criminology, the study of the law breaking, law making, and society's reaction to crime has largely been the study of male law breaking, laws meant to prevent and control male criminality, and study of the punishment of male offenders (Belknap, 2007). Mainstream criminology, in other words, is really what some have termed 'malestream' criminology. The traditional neglect of gender in this field has numerous implications, including the approach we use to manage risk and attempt rehabilitation for offenders in the community.

This book presents findings from a mixed method study of gender and the use of actuarial risk and need assessment instruments for offenders in the correctional system. Two primary questions guide this study – (1) Does one of the most widely used risk and need assessment instruments, the Level of Service Inventory-Revised (LSI-R), exhibit predictive validity for female offenders?; and (2) Does the LSI-R exhibit content validity for female offenders?

In the end, the results do challenge the underlying assumptions of this instrument for females. This presents broader implications for the manner in which we treat female offenders in the criminal justice system, specifically with regard to risk and need assessment instruments. The quantitative analysis of offenders who received an LSI-R assessment demonstrated that the overall predictive validity for male and female offenders was similar, yet there were differences in how male and female offenders scored on the individual domain areas as well as how these domains correlated with recidivism. We would expect the domains, and correlates with recidivism, to look the same for men and women if gender simply did not matter. While predictive validity is essentially the same for males and females in this study, the instrument does not seem to operate in a gender neutral fashion. The alcohol and drug domain alone, for example, was more predictive of female recidivism than was the entire LSI-R score, suggesting that the instrument is indeed affected by serious content validity issues.

Women and men serving time on probation and parole were interviewed extensively regarding items measured by the standardized LSI-R instrument and, additionally, gender-specific factors that were not included. The results of these interviews call into question the content validity of the LSI-R, and similar instruments, for female offenders. The aggregate analyses of the male and female interview data demonstrate the significance of context as well as the potential implications of denying differential gendered context in 'objective' criminogenic risk and need instruments. Of particular importance, factors relevant to female offenders, especially past and present victimization, are left out. The effects of trauma are somewhat reflected in the alcohol and drug domain, yet the true meaning of females' substance abuse problems are masked by these standardized measures. For example, the women routinely stated that they used alcohol and drugs as escape mechanisms and self-medication while the men voiced their usage in the desire to hang out with friends and have fun.

The context of the onset and continuation of alcohol and drug abuse will not be captured in this and similar instruments. As such, women's real issues are essentially hidden in plain sight. In other words, there exists the appearance of gender-neutrality but deeper analysis reveals that this is unfortunately not the case. Many who do claim gender-neutrality rely on the studies of predictive validity, such as this one, that demonstrate similar predictive capability of the LSI-R for males and females. But, it is imperative to keep in mind the domain and contextual gender differences that the qualitative data illustrate. Since these newer risk and need instruments contain criminogenic risks and needs, they are designed to both manage (via risk factors) and treat (via criminogenic needs) offenders in ways that should serve to reduce the likelihood of recidivism. The results from this research call into question the efficacy of this task – at least for female offenders. In terms of treatment, their use may be limited because female offenders' risk often masks the actual underlying root causes of their criminal offending – primarily centered on victimization issues.

These data thus indicate a fundamental problem with the LSI-R for women. Namely, although predictive validity does exist, the questionable content validity for women, compared to men, suggests that the tool will not be as useful for the female offender in terms of positively affecting her level of recidivism and reducing criminogenic needs via the LSI-R outcomes. The findings in this research also suggest that the LSI-R actually penalizes women via higher overall scores, thus higher risk classification, for behavior such as seeking help with drug abuse and trauma issues. This pattern was revealed in the qualitative data but hidden behind the quantitative measures. For example, many women seek mental health treatment for substance abuse and draw social assistance in the process. Women thus are scored higher for seeking mental health treatment and drawing social assistance at a time when they are generally unemployed. They are, in short, penalized by (and in spite of) attempting to heal and become pro-social. On the other hand, troubled intimate relationships are likely to be missed for female offenders, at least as currently measured.

Ultimately the lack of challenge to the epistemology behind which current generations of risk and need assessments lie is yet another chapter in the long standing neglect of placing gender squarely in the center of analyses and practices that directly affect women's criminal justice trajectories. The current gender-neutral (read male-based) risk and need instruments count risk out of its important context and, as a result, misrepresent the meaning of risk for female offenders. In the end, the results challenge us to reconsider the manner in which these types of instruments are created and utilized for female offenders.

How Gender Matters

Careful study of male and female offenders reveals both similarities *and* differences in the context of offending. Yet, as the opening quote of this chapter alludes, the traditional view of many in society has been that human behavior is mainly male behavior and that women simply imitate or act in secondary fashion to their male counterparts (Belknap, 2007). This sentiment has certainly been historically echoed in criminological research. Women have often been neglected in samples of data collection and analyses meant to assess why individuals commit crime, factors that go into sentencing, and other matters related to criminology and the criminal justice system. However, contemporary researchers have made great strides in revealing the nature and extent of female offending.

Women and girls in the criminal justice system have been a hidden population, first and foremost, owing to their smaller numbers relative to their male counterparts (Belknap, 2007; Flavin & Desauls, 2006; Owen, 2003; McLvor et al., 2004; Somers et al., 2006; Holtfreter et al., 2004; Bloom et al., 2003). Female offenders represent roughly:

- 24% of all arrests (Federal Bureau of Investigation, 2008);
- 13% of the total U.S. jail population (Sabol & Minton, 2008);
- 24% of the total U.S. probation population (Glaze & Bonczar, 2007);
- 12% of the total U.S. parole population (Glaze & Bonczar, 2007);
- 7% of the U.S. prison population (Sabol & Couture, 2008);
- and 2% of those on death row (Snell, 2006).

While men still significantly outnumber women in all areas of the system, women are nonetheless making up a growing segment of the population. Indeed, female offenders mark the fastest growing segment of the criminal justice system, especially in corrections (Hannah-Moffat, 2009; Van Voorhis et al., 2008; Holtfreter & Cupp, 2007; Holsinger & Van Voorhis, 2005; Glaze & Bonczar, 2007; Sabol & Couture, 2008; Bloom et al., 2003). Yet, many of the policies and procedures that have been developed to deal with boys and men have been merely applied to girls and women, sometimes with negative, unintended consequences for the latter group.

It is intriguing that gender has been such a neglected aspect of this field given that gender consistently proves to be one of the strongest predictors of criminal offending (Olson et al., 2003; Flavin & Desautels, 2006; Belknap, 2007). Ignoring gender has been a detriment to our understanding of female offenders, for sure, but also in understanding male criminality. In other words, we could learn a lot about male offending (such as why males commit the most crime) via greater study of female offending (why females commit the least crime) (Flavin & Desautels, 2006).

Feminist scholars have made great in-roads in repairing the traditional gender neglect in this field, especially since the 1970's (Belknap, 2007). The most common attempts to include gender have been to take existing theories, existing methods, etc. and to simply 'add gender and stir' (Belknap, 2007; Flavin & Desautels, 2006). The problem with this approach is that we miss challenging the assumptions of original theories or methodologies when we add women as a variable into research or practice based on boys or men.

More attention has recently been paid to the areas in which women are over- or under-represented relative to men. This approach tends to highlight the invisibility of women. Since we are still comparing women to men, though, we are assuming male as the norm against which all else should be compared (Belknap, 2007; Flavin & Desautels, 2006). If there is such a thing as a 'gold standard' in the study of female offenders, it would be to start with women first. Theory, research methods, and samples that serve to focus on the female offender ought to start with gender in mind. We need to study women "on their own terms" (Flavin & Desautels, 2006).

Challenging the Past: Gender Matters & Feminist Epistemology

Issues of gender and sex permeate multiple institutions and perceptions in society, and therefore, taken-for-granted assumptions become ever more important when issues of liberty and punishment are at the fore (Morash, 2005). It is instructive to view gender as an organizing construct for various facets of social institutions, including crime and punishment. Indeed, Sprague (2005, pg.29) suggests that gender is, "…a whole set of social relations that organize us into different social positions with different advantages and constraints based on our sexual preferences and our parental status." As criminologists, it is important that we critically assess the practical ways in which gender truly matters. This is especially true when we examine the manner in which gender, as a structural organizing concept, shapes and influences the lives of individuals under control of the criminal justice system.

As we theorize and craft criminal justice practices it is crucial that we also understand that gender is much more than a simple dichotomy of male and female. Thinking of gender as analogous to sex (male, female) artificially narrows the lens through which we could more thoughtfully understand the macro-level sociological factors that shape the nature and extent of offending - for both males and females. After all, if there were no gender differences, other than biological ones, we would expect there to be a roughly 50/50 split in the population of males and females arrested, sentenced to probation, jail, or prison, released to parole, or sentenced to death. Yet, referring to the numbers listed earlier, we see that this is not the case. Covington & Bloom (2003, pg. 5) further remind us:

> While sex differences are biologically determined, gender differences are socially constructed: they are assigned by society, and they relate to expected social roles. They are neither innate nor unchangeable. Gender is about the reality of women's lives and the contexts in which women live.

Again, when we choose to ignore gender and treat females as men we, in essence, leave these very important contexts hidden. However, the complexity and the content of the female life are often at the root of her involvement in the system and, thus, deserve attention here.

The notion of feminist epistemology, or any epistemology for that matter, forces us to confront the state of existing knowledge. It is only within the past 30 years that serious challenges have been made to the epistemological foundations of existing criminological knowledge and theory. We can now acknowledge that science is *not* value-neutral (Sprague, 2005; Flavin & Desautels, 2006), and, as such, may be biased in significant ways.

The neglect of a gendered lens in criminological research is the result of either intentional neglect or empirical circumstances (Sprague, 2005). Gender simply has not been generally considered as a conceptual problem in conducting research in the field of criminology and criminal justice. Regardless of the milestones from the past 30 years, there is a documented need to continue to impose a feminist standpoint to contemporary criminological research that will, especially, impact the lives of people in the criminal justice system in significant and important ways. Sprague (2005, pg. 80) wisely asks us to consider the following regarding standpoint epistemology, "It poses political questions for each scholar: whose questions do we ask; from whose lives, needs, and interests do we begin; whose ordering of experience do we take seriously; to whom are we responsible to communicate; when has a question been adequately answered?"

The general lack of a feminist standpoint, historically, in criminological theory and research has certainly contributed to gender bias – especially regarding the manner in which we think about the nature and extent of offending. Indeed, this book is ultimately concerned with how this gender bias impacts risk and need assessment instruments. First, though, it remains important to outline why gender should be thoughtfully conceptualized in criminological studies and later policy and practice. It is instructive to turn attention to some of the problems with traditional theoretical frameworks that have clouded the lens through which we understand and conceptualize issues of crime and justice.

While we have traditionally neglected female offenders in theory and research, we have not neglected to generalize male-based constructs and findings to them. Most major criminological theories – such as strain theory, social control theory, social disorganization, and social learning theory, for example - explain criminal offending in terms of some manner of micro and/or macro-level processes that intersect with the offender's life. These theories have long standing empirical support. The "problem" with these theories, though, is that they are mainly built upon knowledge of male offending (Gilfus, 2006; Reisig et al., 2006; Belknap and Holsinger, 2006; McLvor, et al., 2004; Covington & Bloom, 2003; Olson et al., 2003). Indeed, much of the research utilized for the above-mentioned and other existing mainstream explanations of criminal offending are based on male-only samples (Sommers et al., 2006; Sampson & Laub, 2005a; Belknap, 2001; Bloom et al., 2003; Gelsthorpe, 2004), or samples in which females were not analyzed separately from men.

The benefit of including gender should not be understated. Much can be gained from a feminist perspective or a focus on gender. In fact, the attention of feminist scholars gave rise to masculinities research. We have learned much about the violent victimization by men towards men and women via this specific attention to gender.

Misunderstanding to 'Benign Neglect'

At mid-year 2009, we now know quite a bit about the gendered nature and context of offending (Maurutto & Hannah-Moffat, 2007), yet these factors still tend to be largely neglected at best or ignored at worst by mainstream criminology (Belknap & Holsinger, 2006). Unfortunately, a lack of focus on gender-specific (read female) attributes of criminal offending ultimately bias other areas of theory, research (Sommers et al., 2006) and practice. Indeed, the distinction between male and female offenders becomes even more important as we, as standard practice, choose to take theoretical knowledge from male-based theories of offending and attempt to calculate a score that designates risk for re-offending as well as treatment needs and is then applied to *both* female and male offenders (the next chapter will go into greater detail about the nature of these scores, as they relate to risk/need instruments and the implications for ignoring gendered risk factors).

So what do we know about female offenders? As mentioned earlier, one constant factor in criminology is that women commit far fewer crimes than men. So what is it about 'doing gender' that adds to a pool of offenders that is largely male? Feminist research has contributed to our knowledge base regarding both female offending as well as male offending, especially with regard to masculinity (Messerschmidt, 2000; Hagedorn, 1998) and violent crime.

Issues of masculinity not only affect the quantity of crime, but also affect the quality of crime. For example, Miller (2004) found that while both the men and women in her study committed street robberies (a traditionally male crime) for the same reasons, issues of masculinity shaped the manner in which this crime was carried out. Miller notes that (pg. 63) "…the differences that emerge reflected practical choices made in the context of a gender stratified environment in which, on the whole, males are perceived as strong and women are perceived as weak." Similar phenomena can be seen in other work detailing the nature and extent of crime, particularly violent crime, and the manifestation of expected gendered action (Bourgois, 2002; Anderson, 1999; Hagedorn, 1998). The expression of violence, machismo, bravado, and other similar adjectives used to describe male violence is further exacerbated by a cultural norm of hegemonic masculinity (Messerschmidt, 2000) which glorifies, in many respects, male aggression.

Ultimately, a gendered social structure affects both male and female socialization which, in turn, shapes the nature and extent of offending by members of both groups (Flowers, 2003; Hagedorn, 1998). Of course, these issues are further produced by culture and by class (Bourgois, 2002; Anderson, 1999). Indeed, some have argued that within certain subcultures, expressions of violence and crime by men reflect the need to express masculinity and, unfortunately, criminal outlets are the only mechanism for groups otherwise shut out of the mainstream society to do so (Jones, 2006).

Female Offenders and Management Responses 9

While the focus on masculinities is an important one, this research nonetheless takes a decidedly female-centered perspective on female offending and the nature of actuarial risk and need assessment instruments. As stated earlier, most existing theories of criminal offending center on what we know about male patterns and pathways to crime, and masculinity research has helped define how gender, namely male gender, has been affected by societal expectations, peer groups, and a code of the street (Anderson, 1999) that, in the main, demands masculinity from men and femininity from women. Although not inclusive of all feminist theoretical constructs, this work draws from the pathways perspective on female offending. In contrast to the mainstream theories mentioned earlier, this theory is important in detailing the contextual differences in male versus female criminal offending. The importance of this context is ultimately pertinent in framing problems associated with the neglect of gendered-offending differences.

Theorizing Gender: Pathways Perspective

The pathways perspective, in comparison to traditional male-based theories, offers an alternative understanding to female offending than the traditional male based ones. The pathways perspective demonstrates greater theoretical explanatory power for female offender crime trajectories because it incorporates gendered differences in risk factors (Belknap and Holsinger, 2006; Smith, 2002) as well as the manner in which the lives of girls in the criminal justice system are shaped differently than boys (Chesney-Lind, 1997; Bloom et al., 2003). Simply put, female offenders have pathways to crime that are distinctive from those of their male counterparts (Van Voorhis et al., 2008).

Female offender pathways research suggests that, relative to males, females are more likely to be (or have) (McDiarmid, 2005; Bloom et al., 2003; Bloom & Owen, 2002): women of color; in their early- to mid-thirties; convicted of drug or drug-related offenses; have fragmented family histories, with other family members also involved with the criminal justice system; survivors of physical and/or sexual abuse as children and adults; significant substance abuse problems; multiple physical and mental health problems; unmarried mothers of minor children; high school degree/GED, but limited vocational training and sporadic work histories.

Victimization is especially salient to any understanding of female criminality. Abuse in the home, for both juveniles and adults, is theoretically related to criminal offending (Van Voorhis et al., 2008; Belknap & Holsinger, 2006; Reisig et al.; 2006, Bloom et al., 2003; Parsons & Warner-Robbins, 2002; Chesney-Lind, 1997). Females are more likely to be victims of emotional, physical, and/or sexual abuse (Morash, 2005). Thus, females are more likely than males to act in a delinquent or criminal manner in relation or response to this abuse - including substance use, illegal or otherwise. This theory supports the greater number of female runaways (Gilfus, 2006) and the greater percentage of homicides committed by females against intimate partners than that of men. Bloom et al. (2003, pg. 8) note that, "Women's most common pathways to crime involve survival efforts that result from abuse, poverty, and substance abuse." Many women in the criminal justice system are substance abusers or addicts, and research has established a connection between histories of abuse and substance use (Comack, 2006; Hollin & Palmer, 2006; Bloom et al., 2003). There is not only a difference in sexual and physical abuse histories, but also the degree to which childhood abuse for women continues into their adult lives (Chesney-Lind, 2000).

Further, not only are women more likely to have past, present, or a combination of past and present victimization, but, it is also "notable that abused and neglected girls were more likely than non-abused/neglected girls to be arrested for violent delinquency offenses, whereas abused and neglected boys were no more likely to have violent delinquency offense arrests than non-abused/neglected boys" (Belknap and Holsinger, 2006, citing Widom). This again reinforces the idea that gender matters as a socially organizing construct.

Female offenders are also more likely than their male counterparts to have a history of mental illness, substance abuse, and trauma that *precedes* their entry into the criminal justice system (Van Voorhis et al., 2008; Ditton, 1999; Bloom et al., 2003). Typically, the higher rates of depression and post-traumatic stress disorder that women offenders exhibit can be linked to the histories of abuse noted above (Bloom et al., 2003; Lawrence et al. 2004; Farr, 2000; Kruttschnitt and Gartner, 2003). In addition to mental conditions, female offenders are also more likely than their male counterparts to have physical impairments (Kruttschnitt and Gartner, 2003).

Female offenders are more likely than male offenders to have grown up in a single-parent home (Bloom et al., 2003); however, the extent of any causal relationship, in conjunction with the above-mentioned factors, is unknown. There may also be factors that are different for women in their pathways to reintegration. For example, existing literature suggests that the role of motherhood may impact women's attempts to reintegrate into the community from prison (Farr, 2000), as well as their health, issues of Post-Traumatic Stress Disorder, and the impact of competing demands (Richie, 2001). Regardless, female offenders are likely to have been alienated from conventional institutions within society, such as school, legitimate employment, and in-tact families (Bloom et al., 2003). Further, female offenders are much more likely than male offenders to exhibit associations between their personal offending and their relationships with 'bad men,' significant others involved in the criminal justice system, or with those who use or sell drugs (Daly, 1984; Bloom et al., 2003).

Women's pathways to offending are, quite simply, different from those of men - even if allowing from some overlap (Belknap and Holsinger, 2006; Bloom et al., 2003; Modley, 2000; Chesney-Lind, 1997). The pathways approach explains how girls' lives help shape their adult criminal justice involvement. The previous discussion has outlined the important problems that female offenders bring into the criminal justice system. Especially important is evidence that suggests a link between their current involvement in criminal offending and both their childhood and adulthood victimization (Comack, 2006; Hollin & Palmer, 2006; Chesney-Lind & Pasko, 2004). For example, the large number of status offenses for juvenile girls is indicative of troubled lives, such as living in abusive households. Running away from home is a survival strategy for many girls that becomes, despite the technicalities, a criminally sanctioned event (Gilfus, 2006; Chesney-Lind & Pasko, 2004). In short, gender matters in the criminal justice system because gender matters in every other social institution.

The socialization of girls and women, including that centered on patriarchy, shapes the (perceived) available opportunities for girls, and women, who do *not* find themselves on the fringe of society. For those women, however, who *do* find themselves either on the fringe of society, or whose history is marred with troubling family and other relationships, the factors that line their pathways into the criminal justice system should not be ignored. The cumulative nature of research that has framed this approach aligns with broader issues of feminist theory "which is actually not one but several theories that consider the disadvantages and oppression faced by girls and women and emphasizes research that will reduce this oppression" (Morash, 2005, pg. 1).

Many of the factors that contemporary research has determined to be important for female offenders, though, have been largely left out of or ignored in the growth of current instruments designed to both assess for risk of future offending and determine treatment needs for offenders in the criminal justice system. The feminist pathways approach to understanding and making sense of female criminality "offers a better understanding of offender girls' and women's risk factors and needs for interventions and treatment" (Belknap and Holsinger, 2006) and for policy and practice (Bloom et al., 2003). Thus, this is the theoretical framework guiding the work that follows and which, in turn, ultimately aids in the explanation of how, "context, individual interactions, and individual characteristics come together to explain crime and justice" (Morash, 2005, pg. 2).

Correctional Growth and Risk/Need Assessment Instruments

A greater understanding of the context of female offending via the pathways to criminality is increasingly important as the rate of female involvement in the criminal justice system, especially in correctional populations, continues to grow. Again, the growth of the female correctional population has *outpaced* that of males in the system, yet the sheer number of male offenders relative to females tends to hide their rate of growth.

The total U.S. incarcerated population grew 1.8% during 2007 while Hawai'i's prison population increased 0.2% during this time (West & Sabol, 2008). The average annual change in Hawai'i from 2000 – 2006 was 2.8%, compared to 2.0% for the nation. Hawai'i witnessed an increase in its probation population by 10.5% and 9.3% in the parole population in 2006 (Glaze & Bonzcar, 2007). The average change in the female incarcerated population from 2000 through 2006 was 3.4% compared to 2.0% for males (West & Sabol, 2008).

Additionally, 12.5% of the prison population in Hawai'i is female[1]; nearly double the national percentage of 7.2% in 2007 (West & Sabol, 2008).

Regardless of how they actually come into the criminal justice system, an increasing number of offenders do enter. The increase in the rate of both male and female community correctional growth over the past 25 years has posed new constraints on supervising agencies. As such, community and institutional agencies across the nation have increased their use of and reliance upon actuarial based instruments to better manage their growing populations (Holtfreter & Cupp, 2007; Vose et al., 2008; Jones, 1999), as well as to enhance the ability to accurately predict who will reoffend (Hudson, 2003; Champion, 1994). In this study, these actuarial risk assessment instruments[2] are generally meant to include the following:

> The use of statistical rather than clinical methods on large datasets to determine different levels of criminal offending associated with one or more group traits, in order (1) to predict past, present, or future criminal behavior and (2) to administer criminal justice outcome (Harcourt, 2007).

The next chapter will go into further detail on both the evolution of these instruments and the additional inclusion of criminogenic needs not included in the above definition.

This research stems from the intersection of the pathways approach to female offending and the increased use of actuarial risk and need instruments in the criminal justice system. The overwhelming majority of actuarial risk and need assessment instruments currently employed were crafted around knowledge of male offending and validated on males – then merely applied to females (Blanchette & Brown, 2006). The major point of inquiry is whether instruments

---

[1] Hawai'i's figures are somewhat confounded in that prisons and jails form an integrated system in Hawai'i. This should be kept in mind when making direct comparisons with national figures.

[2] The following chapter will provide an in-depth review of the history, proliferation, and current use of these types of instruments on correctional populations, especially community correctional populations.

designed on information about and for male offenders are applicable to female offenders. If the pathways perspective on female offending is correct, unmet treatment needs would also suggest that there are gender differences in predictors of reoffending, or recidivism, as well (Stuart and Brice-Baker, 2004). This is an ever-important research arena, as the need exists to look at how risks and needs are, in fact, gendered. Ideally, this type of research should occur *prior* to the initiation of any policies put in place that serve to affect the lives of both men and women in the criminal justice system (Belknap and Holsinger, 2006). Unfortunately, the creation and application of risk and need instruments have assumed a gender-neutral epistemology and, thus, leave behind some flawed underlying assumptions regarding gendered risks and needs.

Conclusion

The traditional neglect of gender in the field of criminology still exists most prominently in actual policy and application. Sometimes the results are non-consequential, other times the result is a more 'benign neglect' of female offenders. Broad gains in gender appropriate treatment can be realized for those who are willing to pay attention to important issues of gender, feminist research, and feminist epistemologies. Indeed, it has been suggested that failure to account for the scope, detail, and depth of feminist theory, methods, and research demonstrates a disregard of the important work of the past 30 years (Hannah-Moffat, 2009).

This book details a specific growth industry in corrections, the use of actuarial based risk and need instruments, used to classify and manage offenders at an aggregative level. Indeed, the widespread use of actuarial risk and need assessment instruments to manage ever growing correctional populations (Harcourt, 2007; Hollin & Palmer, 2006; Loader & Sparks, 2002) has resulted in a reasonable number of studies which explore their effectiveness in the prediction of female offender recidivism, yet the results have been mixed (Funk, 1999; Harer & Langan, 2001; Olson et al., 2003; Holsinger et al., 2003; Holtfreter et al., 2004; Hubbard & Pratt, 2004; Reisig et al., 2006; Dowden & Andrews, 1999; Van Voorhis et al., 2008).

These instruments have proven a valuable tool in aiding correctional administrators and practitioners in assessing risk for management purposes and need for treatment purposes to an ever-growing correctional population. Yet, these instruments have been crafted around knowledge of male offending and, too, most studies detailing their effectiveness have also been based on male samples (Blanchette & Brown, 2006). Indeed, work highlighted by Holtfreter and Cupp (2007) illustrates that the majority of the research used to support the validity of the LSI-R for females has actually been based on males. Only 11 of the 41 empirical studies published from 1986 through 2006 actually reported statistics for female offenders (Holtfreter & Cupp, 2007). Twenty six of these studies, over half, were based on male-only samples, and only 5 included female only samples. This research adds to the growing number of decidedly female-centered studies. The results of this research demonstrate that gender *does* matter. Gender matters with regard to domain differences as well as, and more importantly, content validity.

We still need to further our understanding of women in the system in the first place before we are able to adequately predict factors that might put them at risk for coming back into the system (or those that might keep them out) or the type of programs they need in order to reduce their chances of recidivism. Hopefully this will book will aid in this regard. Chapter 2 outlines the history, growth, implications, and problems associated with the use of actuarial risk and need instruments for the criminal justice population in general, and for female offenders specifically. Most importantly, this chapter identifies the problems that traditional gender neglect poses for the growing population of female offenders.

Chapter 3 details the importance of studying women as women, not merely as compared to a pre-existing male norm. Important issues here include the use of gender as the framework guiding theoretical construction and research rather than merely as a variable. Methodological and sample details from this study are also included.

Chapter 4 details the results of the predictive validity test of a risk and need assessment instrument, one that is most widely used in the United States and abroad, the Level of Service Inventory-Revised (LSI-R). This chapter highlights results from the predictive validity test. Chapter 5 demonstrates the need to hear women's voices via a presentation of the results of in-depth interviews with both male and female offenders serving time in the community (on either parole or felony probation). The data presented in this chapter reveal the importance of risk, correlation, cause, and context in the lives of the female offenders that, in many important respects, differs from their male counterparts.

Chapter 6 makes sense of the findings from the quantitative and qualitative chapters. In the end, this last chapter argues for the need to incorporate the context of female offending into any attempt to assess their risk or needs via a standardized instrument. Failure to account for gendered differences poses significant disadvantages in the application of supervised punishment for female offenders. The growth in the use of risk and need instruments, coupled with the traditional neglect of female centered study, leaves the possibility of greater harm – to the female offender and to public safety. Ultimately the argument is made that attention must be paid to the context of women's offending and, in the main, gender must be accounted for in any punishment related application of these risk/need assessment instruments. Failure to do so renders the unique circumstances and problems of female offenders hidden in plain sight - behind the objective measurement of these actuarial, standardized instruments.

CHAPTER 2

A Brief History of Risk Management & Gender

In Canada, the enthusiasm of the practioners of the craft of risk assessment design borders on the cult. The issues are seen as 'technical'. Conferences are organized to share methodological insights. Notably absent from programmes are persons speaking to issues of ethics, law or systemic implications. The omissions are not mere oversight.
– Ronald Price, 1997.

Men have egos and women have feelings.
– Jimmy, Probationer on Gender Differences.

Correctional Growth and the Use of Actuarial Risk/Need Instruments

Risk management has emerged as one of the primary mechanisms of offender control in the 21st century. Although not a new practice, the current level of risk management procedures is inextricably linked with the growth in the correctional population – both community and institutional. Actuarial based risk (and need) assessment instruments have become the guiding machinery for risk management decisions (Lowenkamp et al., 2001). As the previous chapter suggests, though, the popularity of these instruments within the criminal justice system over the past two decades, coupled with a paucity of attention paid to gender-specific attributes, merits thoughtful discussion. Based on *aggregate* statistics, these instruments guide, and sometimes dictate, in very important ways, the manner in which *individuals* are treated based upon the *groups* that they share certain attributes with.

Actuarial-based risk/need instruments certainly introduce a Pandora's Box of criminal justice related issues: the meaning of risk in the correctional system, causes versus correlates of (re)offending, differences in female and male (re)offending, and the efficacy of and ethics associated with actuarial-based justice. Regardless, the interest in actuarial criminogenic risk/need assessment instruments, although largely present in most states since the 1970s, has gained a renewed importance as correctional populations continue to grow (Brumbaugh et al., 2005) and, more often than not, without much thought given to the issues cited above. Rather, the exponential growth in the system seems to drive practice. At year end 2007, there were 1,598,316 inmates held in state or federal prisons in the United States (West & Sabol, 2008). An additional 5,035,225 individuals were under some form of community correctional supervision at year end 2006 (Glaze & Bonczar, 2007). Much of this overall correctional growth is attributable to deliberate policy changes, including those associated with the 'war on drugs,' rather than any measurable change in offending behavior (Kruttschnitt and Gartner, 2003; Tonry and Petersilia, 1999; Warren, 2008).

As demonstrated in the previous chapter, Hawai'i's situation and correctional population have experienced parallel patterns of growth. The total U.S. incarcerated population grew 1.8% during 2007 while Hawai'i's prison population increased 0.2% during this time (West & Sabol, 2008). The average annual change in Hawai`i from 2000 – 2006 was 2.8%, compared to 2.0% for the nation. Additionally, Hawai'i witnessed an increase in its probation population by 10.5% in 2006 and 9.3% in the parole population witnessed an increase of 9.3% (Glaze & Bonzcar, 2007).

Regardless of national or local correctional populations, we continue to witness historically high levels and continued growth. Indeed, Mauer and Chesney-Lind (2002) purport that, given the large number of offenders behind bars, we now have a social policy that can be termed mass imprisonment. While this is true, it must be stressed that mass imprisonment is part of a larger phenomenon termed the correctional industrial complex, in which many individuals are swept under the control of the criminal justice system, especially as probationers who serve their time in the community.

The financial impact of this growth, or mass imprisonment, for both the male and female offender populations, has been particularly harsh for most states (Warren, 2008). Mauer and Chesney-Lind (2002, pg. 11) summarize this condition as follows: "Corrections costs have been the fastest growing segment of state budgets, and this has meant that virtually all other aspects of spending, including funds for education and social welfare, have been affected in order to accommodate prison expansion." Objective, or actuarial[3], risk/need instruments are increasingly embraced as a means of making the best use of limited resources during a time of seemingly continuous growth in the correctional population (Baird, 2009; Harcourt, 2007; Austin, 2003; Clements, 1996; Holsinger et al., 2001; Lowenkamp et al., 2001; Jones, 1996). These instruments are thought to contribute to public safety via the accurate identification of individuals at greatest risk for recidivism.

This chapter will detail the issues listed above, starting with a definition and history of actuarial risk/need instruments in general and in the criminal justice system specifically. The current utilization of the latest generation of risk/need instruments is outlined, including how, if at all, gender has factored into both the creation and use of these instruments. The use of these risk/need instruments in Hawai'i is also discussed, as well as the possible implications for female offenders.

Calculating Risk – A General Overview

It seems worthwhile to begin this section with a discussion of the meaning and importance of risk itself. According to Douglas (as cited in Loader & Sparks, 2002, pg. 94), risk is not a tangible thing, but is instead a way of thinking. How one thinks about risk is shaped by larger sociological and environmental factors, as well as by political and other ideologies. Regardless, the criminal justice system has increasingly become 'deeply concerned' with the management of risk (Bosworth, 2004) and how various measures of risk are implicated in all areas of the criminal justice system (Champion, 1994; Harcourt, 2007). Harcourt (2007) states that "more and more, we use risk-assessment tools to identify whom to search, when to punish more, and how to administer the penal sanction."

---

[3] Bonta et. al. (2001) define the actuarial approach as (pg. 229), "…the assessment of risk and needs…based upon the objective measurement of factors that have demonstrated an empirical relationship to rule violation and criminal behavior."

Risk in the criminal justice system is typically measured via some form of standardized assessment instrument that first calculates risk based on some pre-set scale. These instruments are typically actuarial-based. The overriding goal of these instruments has been to identify and/or classify individuals based on shared group statistics (Baird, 2009; Gottfredson, 1987; Champion, 1994) that are often related to levels of risk for recidivism or other forms of undesired conduct. An instrument is generally considered valid if it is able to accurately identify the likelihood of individual level outcomes based on shared group characteristics (Austin et al., 2003). In a sense, these instruments can be viewed as a mechanism for statistically profiling individuals. Actuarial risk/need assessment instruments in criminal justice are generally meant to include the following:

> The use of statistical rather than clinical methods on large datasets to determine different levels of criminal offending associated with one or more group traits, in order (1) to predict past, present, or future criminal behavior and (2) to administer criminal justice outcome (Harcourt, 2007, Prologue).

Further, though, is the distinction between risk instruments and need instruments. Although these foci are sometimes contained within one tool, they may also be separated[4]. Champion (1994, pg. 19) gives a useful description of these types of assessments:

> ...risk (or dangerousness) instruments are screening devices intended to distinguish between different types of offenders for purposes of determining initial institutional classification, security placement and inmate management, early release eligibility, and the level of supervision required under conditions of probation or parole. Needs assessment devices are instruments that measure an offenders' personal/social skills, health, well-being, and emotional stability, educational level and vocational strengths and weaknesses, alcohol/drug dependencies, mental ability, and other relevant life factors,

---

[4] Baird (2009) argues that risks and needs should not be combined in one instrument.

and which highlight those areas for which services are available and could or should be provided.

The instruments that fit the definitions cited above will be referred to as risk/need instruments throughout this work. Specifically, the research outlined in this book is primarily related to risk/need instruments as currently utilized in community correctional settings rather than in institutional ones, although there is certainly overlap in these areas.

While the use of these types of risk/need instruments are currently widespread, the question remains at what point in history did we begin to 'empiricize' those women, men, and children who are processed through our justice systems? Unlike other 'sexier' forms of discipline, control, and punishment, risk/need instruments remain a largely hidden method of controlling offenders. Neither the public nor politicians, and sometimes criminal justice workers, understand the rationale behind their use, nor do they necessarily trust their use over and above their own human judgment. Although this particular aspect is not the focus of this study, this mechanism of control deserves attention because it affects so many of our offenders, both in the community as well as within correctional institutions.

Foucault (1977) provides perhaps the best description of the beginnings of a science-based criminal justice system, as well as the rationale for such a system. He argues that one of the goals of the criminal justice system, post the public-execution and torture era, was to punish. Indeed, Foucault argues that the criminal justice system set about to punish not for revenge, but to simply punish better, not necessarily less. According to Foucault, the 18th century marked a move from arbitrary punishments toward one in which there was a focus on homogenizing the application of punishment. While Foucault was clearly discussing the actual application of punishment, the use of actuarial risk/need instruments to identify classes of offenders is clearly a way of homogenizing how punishment is applied, as well as when and to whom such punishment is applied. Indeed, the crux of these risk/need instruments is the treatment of individual offenders according to their similarities with others who share similar 'risky' attributes. In a similar vein, Foucault notes the following (1977, pg. 138):

> …it might be said that discipline creates out of the bodies it controls four types of individuality, or rather an individuality

that is endowed with four characteristics: it is cellular (by the playoff of spatial distribution), it is organic (by the coding of activities), it is genetic (by the accumulation of time), it is combinatory (by the composition of forces). And in doing so, it operates four great techniques: it draws up tables; it prescribes movements; it imposes exercises; lastly, in order to obtain the combination of forces, it arranges 'tactics'.

This shift in correctional practice, from a focus on the body to a focus on the mind, was one that was less about punishing in a punitive manner so much as one that focused on fixing or correcting individuals to produce normal (e.g., mainstream) and socially-conformative individuals.

Yet, some have argued that as we moved to the use of actuarial risk/need instruments, we began to engage in a new penology that demonstrated a shift from treating offenders as individuals to one that treats them as part of a population with whom they share aggregate characteristics (Feeley and Simon, 1992; Harcourt, 2007; Smith et al., 2009). It is argued that this, in turn, affected the manner in which these individuals were treated. Rather than trying to produce conformity through normalization (Simon, 1993), there was an increased utilization of incarceration, mass surveillance, and the overall containment of offenders (Feeley and Simon, 1992). This coincided with the emergence of a pervasive concern with risk management (Bosworth, 2004). With this shift to risk management evolved a criminal justice system, theoretically, that was less concerned with any type of ethical or moral obligation to rehabilitate offenders, and was more concerned with controlling and managing a dangerous and risky class of offenders (Feeley and Simon, 1992; Simon, 1993; and Bosworth, 2004).

An interesting critique of the current actuarial approach stems from Harcourt (2007). Harcourt ultimately argues against prediction for three primary reasons. First, he argues that actuarial instruments serve to increase, rather than decrease, criminal offending. Second, Harcourt argues that by defining constructs and objectively identifying certain groups we ultimately serve to increase the very carceral population that we seek to reduce. The profiled group becomes larger than the non-profiled but nonetheless offending group. Risk identification is thus not spread evenly. Finally, Harcourt argues that the actuarial approach serves to distort our conceptions of justice and ultimately changes the entire manner in which we conceptualize justice.

Traditionally, the actuarial movement is associated with the management of individuals via characteristics they share with a larger aggregate population. Newer risk/need instruments, third generation ones (discussed further in the following section), coupled with the risk principle[5], suggests that you actually get both aggregate and individual level focus. In other words, the newer risk/need instruments still classify individuals based on how closely they align with members of a larger aggregate group. However, individuals are then, theoretically, guided into individualized treatment based on their risk/need assessment scores generally, and specifically within the domains, or subscales, in which they score highest. Hannah-Moffat and Shaw (2003) note that the movement towards the use of risk/need instruments is a "contemporary manifestation of two older concerns: predicting dangerousness of re-offending and determining "what works" and "what is needed" in terms of correctional program interventions. These instruments are increasingly used in jurisdictions as case management tools to deliver and guide treatment, especially within probation and parole (Brumbaugh et al., 2005). As such, this renders the Feeley and Simon (1992) notion of a new penology somewhat problematic.

Nonetheless, the history of risk as a criminological concept is not a new one, yet it has gained popularity as a theoretical and practical concept within criminology and criminal justice, especially within the past 20 years (Hollin & Palmer, 2006; Loader & Sparks, 2002) and equally important as an avenue of research. Issues of prediction occupy a significant contemporary space beyond criminal justice; indeed, the use of prediction in decision-making across behavioral and other sciences cannot be understated (Gottfredson & Snyder, 2005).

Advocates of actuarial-based systems of decision-making indicate that they increase effectiveness in managing offenders (Holsinger et al., 2001) and, consequently, increase public safety (Smith et al., 2009; Blanchette & Brown, 2006). One of the major purported benefits, then, of actuarial risk/need instruments is the substitution of gut feelings for

---

[5] The risk principle is a concept that essentially means to target programs and rehabilitation towards the highest risk offenders in order to receive the greatest reductions in recidivism (Van Voorhis, 2005).

objective, or informed, decision-making. Discussions in this area have focused on clinical versus objective judgments. There is much research to suggest that decisions based upon, or informed by, actuarial instruments are significantly more accurate than those based on clinical judgment alone (Bonta, 2002; Holtfreter & Cupp, 2007; Holsinger et al., 2001; Simon, 1993; Gottfredson, 1987). The basic issue here centers on the idea that advanced statistical modeling can factor in the many variables related to a specific criterion in a way that the human mind cannot. Further, there is the argument that the human mind has a tendency to subjectively bias what is and is not factored into any decision-making equation (Holtfreter & Cupp, 2007).

However, there are concerns with the use of risk/need instruments in criminology. Theoretically, actuarial risk/need instruments promote objectively informed decisions that can be applied to entire populations (Holsinger et al., 2001). However, ours is not a perfect science, hence there is necessarily the introduction of error in any prediction stemming from actuarial risk/need-based assessments. Again, the best we can currently hope to achieve in terms of predictive accuracy is about 70 percent (Holsinger et al., 2001). This, in turn, means that false negatives (e.g., predicting someone will be unsuccessful when they actually are successful) and false positives (e.g., predicting someone will be successful when they actually are not) will occur about 30% of the time. It is also quite possible to bias the variables and samples that constitute the original statistical model building[6]. Issues of error and bias that are endemic in the construction and application of these risk/need instruments certainly raise questions about their ethical usage. It is useful to first discuss the history of risk/need instruments to demonstrate why this might be the case.

The Evolution of Actuarial Risk/Need Instruments in Criminal Justice

As stated earlier, actuarial-based assessments have been used for many years in many facets of life, such as in the health and automobile insurance fields, or as tests of creditworthiness. The field of criminal justice generally, and community corrections specifically, is no different in this regard (Harcourt, 2007; Bosworth, 2004; Champion,

---

[6] Leaving out gender-specific variables is one example of one such potential bias. This issue will be explored further in this chapter.

1994; Gottfredson, 1987). Indeed, correctional agencies are chiefly concerned with the management of risk (Blanchette & Brown, 2006) as this relates directly to public safety.

The earliest American use of a classification system in criminal justice appears to be the system used for the classifying and separating inmates in the Walnut Street Jail in the 18th century (Champion, 1994). By most accounts, though, the evolution of actuarial-based risk assessments begins with Bruce in 1928 (Smith et al., 2009; Holsinger et al., 2001) who designed an instrument to predict recidivism. The instrument designed by Bruce was based on the records of 3,000 parolees in Illinois. Ernest Burgess followed not long after, and, in fact, most actuarial risk/need instruments actually utilize the so-called Burgess method of scoring, in which risk factors are merely dichotomized to represent the presence or absence of a factor. Following the seminal work of Bruce and Burgess, assessment instruments were developed in a multitude of criminal justice arenas in order to help guide decision-making, including parole and bail release, sentencing, and prosecution[7] (Holsinger et al., 2001; Champion, 1994).

Although Bruce and Burgess each devised actuarial risk prediction instruments in the 1920s (Zamble & Quinsey, 2001; Gottfredson & Gottfredson, 1985), as did Ohlin in the 1950s (Farrington & Tarling, 1985), the earliest risk and need assessment instruments to receive widespread use in the field of corrections date back to the 1970s. These are now referred to as first generation risk/need assessment instruments.

These first generation instruments were largely clinical-based, subjective assessments of individuals, upon which some sort of treatment plan was devised (Van Voorhis, 2005; Bonta, 1996; Gottfredson, 1987). These decisions, though, were largely made by practitioners and were based upon their own personal experience and the utilization of 'gut level' decision-making (Van Voorhis, 2005). A major critique of these instruments is that the subjective basis of their application inevitably led to the inconsistent treatment of offenders (Van Voorhis, 2005). As such, they also become invalid as overall

---

[7] See Harcourt (2007) for a thorough review of criminal justice risk and need instruments.

predictors of recidivism because they were far too inaccurate (Van Voorhis, 2005).

A second generation of assessment tools marked an improvement over the first (Bonta, 1996). These instruments were widely used in the 1980s (Champion, 1994). Second generation instruments were designed to be objective in nature, empirically based (Van Voorhis, 2005), and largely utilized information known at the time of assessment. In other words, the factors that were scored were static. Static factors represent ones that were historical in nature and, accordingly, were not connected to any type of treatment plans or goals (Bonta, 1996; Van Voorhis, 2005). These historical factors were not considered changeable and, thus, could not be utilized as targets for treatment.

In the 1990s, a critique of the arbitrariousness with which offenders were dealt with and classified led to a refocus on objective actuarial risk/need instruments for offenders (Clear, 2003; Clements, 1996). This contemporary refocusing on risk/need instruments has centered on the creation and use of third generation risk/need assessment tools. Third generation instruments moved beyond the second generation (Van Voorhis, 2005) by including both static and dynamic factors (Bonta, 1996) in the assessment of risk and need, and were designed to aid in the rehabilitation process (Smith et al., 2009). As mentioned earlier, while there is still, and always will be, error, the newer instruments are about 70% accurate. Additionally, even with error, these instruments are more accurate than judgment alone (Gottfredson, 1987) and do help balance the unfettered discretion that can also result in biased criminal justice decision-making (Petersilia, 2003). Bonta (2002) also notes that correlations with recidivism (sexual) were $r = .10$ for clinical versus $r = .46$ for actuarial based assessments. Finally, these newer instruments also begin with theory (Bonta, 2002) which marks considerable improvement over past generations.

The inclusion of dynamic factors, or factors that are changeable, is what allows for the crafting of case management, or a treatment plan, and marks these third generation risk/need assessment instruments as different than previous ones (Van Voorhis, 2005; Hannah-Moffat & Shaw, 2003). The static factors are typically referred to as the risks while the dynamic factors are typically referred to as criminogenic needs. According to Bonta (1996, pg. 23), "Criminogenic needs [the dynamic factors] are linked to criminal behavior. If we alter these needs, then we challenge the likelihood of criminal behavior. Thus criminogenic needs are actually risk predictors, but they are dynamic in nature rather than static." Theoretically, this newer generation of instruments provides the simultaneous ability to predict as well as to reduce the likelihood of recidivism (Andrews & Bonta, 2000; Jones, 1999). Additionally, the predictive ability of an instrument improves if both static and dynamic factors are included (Van Voorhis et al., 2008; Petersilia, 2003). Yet, even though the research has demonstrated that the current instruments are able to predict who will recidivate at about 70% accuracy when both static and dynamic factors are included, a large amount of variation in offending is left unexplained[8].

To reiterate an earlier point, the nature of these third generation risk/need instruments counters the idea of 'the new penology' in community corrections (Feely & Simon, 1992). They do so because the intent behind these new actuarial risk/need instruments moves beyond mere risk classification and toward a method of *both* classification and needs assessment for the explicit purpose of individual treatment intervention (Bonta, 2002). It is, however, an unlikely marriage of group attributes identifying offenders for individual-level treatment.

There is, nonetheless, a large body of literature concerning the factors that are strongly and positively correlated with recidivism (Zamble and Quinsey, 2001). Yet, these are predominantly restricted to what we know about male offending (Hollin & Palmer, 2006; Fagan et al., 2007; Farrington & Painter, 2004). The majority of instruments in use today virtually ignore gender-specific variables otherwise informed via the pathways perspective or other gendered theoretical literature (Hannah-Moffat, 2009; Van Voorhis et al., 2008; Maurutto & Hannah-Moffat, 2007; Deschenes et al., 2006; Reisig et al., 2006). Bosworth (2004) identifies the following problem with risk/need instruments as currently designed: "....quite aside from the critique that may be made of the nature and limited vision of such instruments, it has become increasingly problematic that so few differentiate between offenders on the basis of socioeconomic factors like gender, race, class, or

---

[8] With the highest correlations with outcome at about r=.35, only about 12% of the variance in recidivism is really explained. However, the instruments were not designed to explain recidivism. Rather, the purpose, in part, is to predict its occurrence.

sexuality." These issues will be explored further in the following section.

From a very practical standpoint, the proliferation of actuarial justice, or the use of actuarial risk/need assessment instruments, lies in the efficacy of these probabilistic models (Loader & Sparks, 2002). Indeed, the goal of these actuarial risk/need instruments is to predict, as accurately as possible, an outcome (Gottfredson & Synder, 2005) better than clinical judgment alone (Gottfredson, 1987). Given these criteria, it is important to look at *how* and *how well* these instruments have predicted outcome generally, and with female offenders specifically.

As currently designed, the theoretical application of third-generation risk/need assessments do pose problems for the idea of a new penology, yet are still tied to Foucault's notions of fixing the individual rather than punishing the body. Hannah-Moffat & Shaw (2003, pg. 60) note that the recent trend reflects a hybridization of risk and rehabilitation. It is a "mixed model of government," wherein traditional rehabilitative strategies are reaffirmed and deployed to minimize and reduce risk. It re-establishes a place for rehabilitative regimes in correctional institutions." Unfortunately, though, the evolution of these current risk/need instruments is not complete given the lack of a specific focus on theories of criminality outside traditional male-centered, mainstream criminology. We should use the important literature from the past 20 years to inform these instruments. That same literature demonstrates that certain demographic characteristics, such as gender, do and should matter in the creation and application of risk assessment and should therefore be considered (Maurutto & Hannah-Moffat, 2007; Deschenes et al., 2006).

Gender Matters in the Usage of Third Generation Risk/Need Instruments

The potential problems with actuarial instruments are myriad, and include the validity of their predictions, ethical issues, and the general meaning of risk in criminal justice. Since the goal of these instruments is on accurate predictions and not explanations, there is also often a disconnect between the issues of correlations versus causes. Essentially, by focusing on the prediction side, practitioners have availed themselves of causal behavior and instead focus on correlations with outcome. Do correlations indeed equate to risk and, if not, is it ethical to continue to engage in policy that assumes they do?

Efficacy of actuarial risk/need instruments aside, they have nonetheless been rendered problematic when merged with practice. The disconnect between gendered theory and practice is an important one for many reasons, primarily, though, because risk/need instruments are sold on their theoretical efficiency. Yet, attention to their practical efficiency is often lacking. Additionally, ignoring relevant factors - such as gender - may further damage their validity. As Gottfredson (1987) stated some time ago, there needs to be a theory-driven approach to the prediction problem. And, while current instruments are theory-driven, they are driven by male-centered, mainstream criminological theories. Unfortunately, the application of current instruments to female offenders indicates an attempt to treat female criminality according to constructs defined around male offenders (McLvor et al., 2004) while largely ignoring those relevant to females (Van Voorhis et al., 2008; Bloom et al., 2003).

While actuarial risk/need instruments have proven increasingly reliable and valid in predicting recidivism, the increase in the number of female offenders subject to such assessments poses a renewed problem for the criminal justice system. As the use in actuarial risk/need instruments increases, the implication for their use on female offenders needs to be explored.

To summarize, the majority of research conducted in the area of risk/need assessment instruments has centered on male offenders and was, thus, tailored for men (Hollin & Palmer, 2006; Bloom et al., 2003; Champion, 1994). As presented in Chapter 1, the literature on female offenders suggests that offending, in general, is gendered. The next theoretically logical step is to look at criminogenic risks and needs as gendered as well (Hannah-Moffat & Shaw, 2001; Daly & Chesney-Lind, 1988). In other words, if a classification instrument is based on male offenders, and offending and risk are both gendered, then the same instrument should not automatically be applied to a different gender, namely females. Unfortunately, most, and certainly all mainstream risk/need assessment instruments, have been created and applied without thoughtful consideration of gender generally and female offenders specifically (Holtfreter & Cupp, 2007).

The applicability of correctional methods designed for male offenders has been rendered questionable, especially as the female correctional population continues to outpace that of males. A major critique has been whether it is reasonable to merely apply correctional methods that have been designed and based upon male offending to an increasingly female population (Chesney-Lind, 1998). While some research has discovered no gender differences in risk factors (Farringon & Painter, 2004) most studies have been male-based (Hubbard & Matthews, 2008). The existing research on female recidivism, although slight in comparison to that on males, certainly indicates gendered differences in re-offending (Stuart & Brice-Baker, 2004). This is not factored into current risk/need instruments. Attention to this concept is especially timely as the overall risk posed by women is more often low, and many factors that predict risk for men are invalid as predictors of risk for women (Farr, 2000).

While there may be overlap in gendered risks/needs (Heilbrun et al., 2008; Raynor, 2007), there are certainly areas that are decidedly gendered. Hannah-Moffat and Shaw (2001, pg. 10), in a review of literature, note evidence of:

> ...the different characteristics and experiences of female populations. This includes their child-care responsibilities, health needs, extensive histories of physical and sexual abuse, and the fact that much violence committed by women – unlike men – was in the context of abusive family relationships.

These factors appear to be supported by periodic government-sponsored surveys on the prison population. The latest such survey demonstrates that 46.5% of state prison female inmates had ever been physically abused and 39.0% had ever been sexually abused, compared to male figures of 13.4% and 5.8%, respectively (Harlow, 1999). Similar gender disparities exist for federal prison inmates, jail inmates, and probationers. Commonly cited factors related to offending for females (gender-specific needs) include the following:

- Abuse (sexual and physical) related trauma (Van Voorhis et al., 2008; Hubbard & Matthews, 2008; Holtfreter & Cupp, 2007; Bloom et al., 2003; Reisig et al., 2006; Widom, 1995; Chesney-Lind & Pasko, 2004; Hollin & Palmer, 2006);
- Childcare needs (Van Voorhis et al., 2008; Holtfreter & Cupp, 2007; Hollin & Palmer, 2006; Bloom et al., 2003);

- Mental health problems (Van Voorhis et al., 2008; Hubbard & Matthews, 2008; Holtfreter & Cupp, 2007; Hollin & Palmer, 2006);
- Low social capital, including lack of education and employment skills (Holtfreter & Cupp, 2007; Reisig et al., 2006);
- Drug abuse (Holtfreter & Cupp, 2007; Hollin & Palmer, 2006; Reisig et al., 2006);
- Problems with intimate relationships (Van Voorhis et al., 2008); and
- Self-esteem & self-efficacy (Van Voorhis et al., 2008; Hubbard & Matthews, 2008).

Whether or not, how, and to what degree these needs matter in risk/need assessments still warrants greater research effort (Heilbrun et al., 2008; Blanchette & Brown, 2006; Bloom et al., 2003).

Chesney-Lind (2002, pg. 83) affirms that "…gender plays a major role in the forces that propel women into criminal behavior. For this reason, gender must be taken into account in the crafting of effective responses to their problems." Should we believe, for example, that female re-offending behavior (i.e., recidivism) is somehow different from initial offending? This is, essentially, what systematically occurs when we assess the criminogenic risks and needs of women using instruments crafted from research based on men.

As discussed in the previous chapter, existing research suggests that there are gendered predictors of both initial and reoffending behavior, especially with regard to abuse. In a study of adult boot camp graduates, for example, Benda (2005) found that sexual and physical abuse prior to the age of 18 as well as within the two years prior to program completion, in addition to selling drugs, were more positively related to recidivism for female than for male offenders.

The failure of correctional practices to consider women, separate from men, creates largely unexplored implications for the female offender (Covington & Bloom, 2003). Chesney-Lind (2002, pg. 83) poses the following question, "Setting aside the legal aspects of this dispute, will treating women offenders as if they were men result in effective responses to their behavior?" The preliminary answer to this question appears to be no. For example, studies indicate that the lack of validity attached to classification instruments with regard to gender creates a situation whereby women offenders are often over-classified (Van Voorhis et al., 2008; Covington & Bloom, 2003) and potentially under-classified as well. Regardless of errors in over- or under-classification, each type of error has potentially negative implications for the correctional experience of the female offender. Over-classification could result in greater punishment and/or surveillance than warranted (Holtfreter & Cupp, 2007), while under-classification could result in a lack of appropriate supervision and effective treatment intervention.

It is important, at the very least, that instruments be validated on both women and men prior to their use (Covington & Bloom, 2003). Unfortunately, most risk/need assessment instruments are based on what we know about male offending and correlates of recidivism (Van Voorhis et al., 2008; Covington & Bloom, 2003). The validity of these instruments for female offenders has yet to be established because gendered theory and research in this area is not yet robust or meaningful enough. When studies have produced claims of gender-neutrality, though, they are usually faulted on two fronts – they do not disaggregate gender and/or they do not utilize representative samples of female offenders (Holtfreter & Cupp, 2007).

The Level of Service Inventory-Revised (LSI-R)

The third-generation risk/need instrument most widely utilized for both male and female offenders is the Level of Service Inventory-Revised (LSI-R) (Holtfreter & Cupp, 2007; Vose et al., 2008) and is the instrument of focus for this research. The LSI-R is increasingly recognized as the best available risk/need assessment instrument (Smith et al., 2009; Harcourt, 2007). It is one of two instruments designed specifically to measure criminogenic risks and needs (Bonta, 1996). The instrument contains 54 items and is similar to the Burgess method of scoring. For example, the presence of a factor is scored as a 1 and the absence of the risk factor is a 0. The sum of all the scores provides the total, overall risk score. Further, the 54 items contained in the instrument are clustered into 10 different domain areas[9]. In addition

---

[9] The LSI-R contains 10 domains, including: criminal history, education & employment, financial, family & marital, accommodations, leisure &

to the classification of risk level, the instrument is also designed to identify the domain area(s) that is most criminogenic for an individual offender. Those areas deemed most criminogenic should become targets of treatment intervention for the individual offender. Andrews & Bonta (2000) describe, in part, the LSI-R in the following terms:

> The LSI-R is a way of systematically bringing together risk and needs information important to offender treatment planning for assigning levels of freedom and supervision. Many times, people working with offenders are guided by their "intuition," "gut feeling," and professional judgment based on their knowledge and experience with offenders. The use of professional judgment is important and should not be dismissed. However, objective risk/needs offender assessment instruments have some advantages over professional judgment approaches (pg. 1)...

Of course, successful elimination of these criminogenic needs contributes to a total reduction in the risk-needs score. Theoretically, lowering scores on dynamic items through appropriate treatment (level of service), and hence overall risk levels, will lead to a reduction in recidivism.

The LSI (the precursor to the more recent LSI-R) was developed in the 1970s and subsequently validated *on* (versus based upon) females in the late 1980s and early 1990s. This instrument, like most other risk assessment instruments, has simply been developed for males and adopted for women. The LSI-R lacks the specific focus on female offenders in both its construction as well as validation efforts (Holtfreter & Cupp, 2007; Covington & Bloom, 2003). However, some, such as Bonta et al. (2001) seem to indicate that the role of "different" than white male matters little, as evidenced in the following statement, "...the LSI-R has its theoretical basis in the general psychology of criminal conduct and therefore, [is] independent of territorial boundaries and citizenship." In other words, the implication is that since the instrument is psychologically based, differences

---

recreation, companions, alcohol & drug, emotional & personal, and attitudes & orientations.

between genders, and even ethnicities, in terms of crimes committed must merely be manifestations of a similar underlying "incorrect" trait (Smith et al., 2009).

While the literature addressing problems with the LSI-R and other so-called third generation risk/need assessment instruments is relatively sparse, various concerns and critiques have been expressed. The LSI-R was noted as having been "made for men, then validated for women" (Wright, 2002). The LSI-R does contain known correlates of criminogenic risk and need variables related to recidivism, but lacks those variables known to be particularly relevant to female offenders (Van Voorhis, 2005). Although the theoretical base of the LSI-R centers on the psychology of criminal conduct and social learning theory, the debate over whether or not the psychology of female criminal conduct is different from that of men continues. Further, there is an expressed need to re-examine the theoretical assumptions for any classification instrument in terms of subpopulations, such as women and ethno-cultural minorities (Reisig et al., 2006; Hannah-Moffat & Shaw, 2003; Whitaker, 2000). These concerns center on the lack of theoretical attention to female offending and the context within which that occurs (Reisig et al., 2006).

Since few studies have specifically centered on an examination of women's criminogenic risks and needs, separate from those of men (Hollin & Palmer, 2006; Reisig et al., 2006; Holtfreter et al., 2004; Olson et al., 2003; Bloom & Owen, 2002; Funk 1999, Richie, 2001), it is not empirically known whether women's more prevalent histories of physical and/or sexual abuse, mental and physical health problems, and relationship and parental difficulties (as well as other gendered factors) are in fact relevant to current risk/need instruments, such as the LSI-R (Reisig et al., 2006). The literature on female offenders does suggest that higher rates of physical and sexual abuse are implicated in more mental health issues for female offenders, such as anxiety, depression, emotional problems, self-esteem, and substance abuse (Van Voorhis and Presser, 2001), which may be related to an increased risk of recidivism for women, over and above that of men (Richie, 2001).

As mentioned earlier, the LSI-R is based, in large part, on the theoretical concepts developed in social learning theory (Andrews & Bonta, 2000). Social learning theory asserts that criminal behavior is learned through, "complex interactions between cognitive, emotional, personality, and biological factors and environment reward-cost contingencies" (Bonta, 2002). The LSI-R is purported to be the most theoretically robust risk/need instrument, with a focus on the "Big Four" domain areas – criminal history, companions, emotional/personal, and attitudes/orientation (Bonta, 2002). These are the domains thought to be most predictive of recidivism. However, social learning theory is a theory of criminality based upon what we know about male offending and, further, does not consider gender as a socially organizing construct (Morash, 2009; Hubbard & Matthews, 2008). These risk/need instruments should be constructed with females in mind if they are to be used on that population of offenders. Belknap and Holsinger (2006) remind us of this important point:

> First, mainstream theories should incorporate what has been learned from feminist pathways theory in assessing the role of abuse events as delinquency risks for both girls and boys. More specifically, the pathways approach to delinquency risk factors appears to provide the most support for determining not only girls' risks but also boys' risks. Unlike the general strain theory and life-course approaches, the pathways approach specifically advances the need to identify childhood traumas as precursors to delinquency (and adult offending).

Failure to account for these important and documented theoretical differences is a true weakness of current risk/need instruments for female offenders. Ultimately, the failure to account for gender, via theory or otherwise, also represents a failure to account for the myriad ways in gender matters sociologically (e.g., power, earnings, resources, caregivers, etc.) (Morash, 2009; Hubbard & Matthews, 2008; Holtfreter & Cupp, 2007). Mainstream theories, such as social learning, fall short of significantly considering gender and the context within which females commit crime (Holtfreter & Cupp, 2007). Baird (2009) cautions that if we continue to assess via factors that are only slightly or not at all predictive of recidivism then we might actually end up with flawed assessments – surely gender matters in this respect.

Hannah-Moffat and Shaw (2001) note, "To determine, empirically and reliably, if the same factors are relevant for women and in the same ways for men, we need further research" (pg. 18). The answer to the validity for women question is an important one, given that the scores obtained on these "objective" instruments will guide the manner in which offenders are supervised and treated in communities, jails, or prisons, and may additionally be utilized by judges during sentencing[10]. There is a definite need to study the use, impact, and outcome of new instruments on the population for which they are used (Olson et al., 2003; Van Voorhis & Presser, 2001; Funk, 1999; Latessa, 1999). This research will address not only the use, impact, and outcomes of the LSI-R on women in Hawai'i, but also the content validity of the risk/need items contained within the LSI-R for women, as compared to men. This is an especially important implication because, although the pathways to offending are likely not the same for both genders, the correlates of recidivism may be (Hollin & Palmer, 2006). And, too, if we intend to craft treatment responses based on the scores on dynamic items then it is also important that we measure gendered factors that matter (Van Voorhis et al., 2008). To reiterate, problems of over-classification, greater supervision, lack of female-relevant theory, questionable nature of gendered risks and needs render the use of the LSI-R, and similar instruments, problematic (Holtfreter & Cupp, 2007). In the main, the lack of gender in the construction of these risk/need instruments in essence assures that gender difficulties and inequities are blindly built into them (Hannah-Moffat, 2009).

It should also be noted that there is an important need to focus on race, and the interaction of gender, race and class, in actuarial-based outcomes (Bosworth, 2004; Farr, 2000) as well as on the theory that should be used in the development of any risk/need instrument (Gottfredson, 1987). Both race and class are critical elements in reentry and risk to recidivism (Petersilia, 2003). However, this particular research is firmly focused on gender-related correlates of risk to reoffend in terms of the utility of risk/need instruments.

Current Gender-Relevant LSI-R & Risk/Need Instrument Research

This section chiefly examines research conducted on the LSI-R. There exists empirical support for third generation risk/need instruments, including the LSI-R (Smith et al., 2009; Vose et al., 2008). The

---

[10] In Hawai'i, as in other jurisdictions, the results are not used to determine in/out prison decisions or sentence length decisions but are instead utilized to aid in the determination of specific risk factors and treatment needs for post-conviction community supervision or release.

predictive validity of this instrument has been demonstrated for inmate classification (Bonta and Motiuk, 1992; Bonta, 1989). Motiuk et al. (1996) noted the predictive validity of the LSI for a sample (male) of halfway house placements and subsequent outcomes. Yet, while some researchers have found predictive validity for the use of the LSI-R and outcomes (Coulson et al., 1996, Olson et al., 2003), studies were insufficiently definitive to make any claims of scientific validity, which can only be established through multiple studies over time and subjects.

Less attention has been paid to the reliability of the instrument. Austin et al., (2003) discovered that the LSI-R was not reliable and, further, that only 8 of the total 54 LSI-R items actually correlated with recidivism. While these researchers did find that the overall LSI-R score was related to recidivism, they also found that the overall 54 items created too much noise in the actual application of the instrument. The 8 factors that were significant were mainly static ones, calling into question the treatment aspect of this instrument. Austin et al., (2003) discovered greater predictive ability via use of the 8 valid and reliable factors, coupled with some demographic variables. Austin et al., (2003) also caution that perhaps we should go back to the fundamental concept of reliability prior to declaring claims of predictive validity.

While the Austin et al. (2003) caution is critical, and certainly duly noted, it is also important to analyze the practical utility of the instrument as currently used. This is especially true because, as stated earlier, the LSI-R is the most commonly used risk/need instrument and is already in use – for both males and females. As such, it is important to look at salient LSI-R predictive validity and scoring research.

The question remains as to whether or not it makes a difference that these risk/need assessment instruments were created and largely validated based upon male samples and later applied to females (Maurutto & Hannah-Moffat, 2007; Holtfreter & Cupp, 2007). Does gender matter in risk assessment? Or, importantly, *how* does gender matter? The analysis by Holtfreter & Cupp (2007) reveals that care must be given to the review of published studies that assert gender-neutrality. First, different patterns emerge in mixed gender models as compared to single gender, multivariate models, even with the same samples.

Even though there is a wealth of qualitative data regarding the differences between male and female offenders, the answer to whether, in the aggregate, these factors matter in terms of recidivism has yet to be solidified. An increasing number of studies have attempted to empirically address whether there are significant differences in predictors of recidivism for men and women (Bloom et al., 2003; Farr, 2000; Olson et al., 2003, Bloom, 2000; Funk, 1999; Manchak et al., 2009; Smith et al., 2009; Van Voorhis et al., 2008; Veysey & Hamilton, 2007; Fagan et al., 2007). These studies are still relatively low compared to male-based research. Yet, the importance of discovering the predictive ability of gendered factors cannot be understated as these factors are directly implicated in the manner(s) in which offenders are both treated and processed through the system (Hubbard & Pratt, 2004). It is nonetheless important for any predictive instrument to include indicators that have been drawn from theoretical assumptions (Farr, 2000; Farrington & Tarling, 1985).

More poignant is the work highlighted by Holtfreter and Cupp (2007). These researchers discovered that the majority of the research used to support the validity of the LSI-R for females has actually been based on males. Only 11 of the 41 empirical studies published from 1986 through 2006 actually reported statistics for female offenders (Holtfreter & Cupp, 2007). Twenty six of these studies, over half, were based on male-only samples, only 5 included female only samples. Vose et al. (2008) found the LSI-R to be predictive of recidivism for females and males. The LSI-R worked best for mixed samples, followed by male-only and finally female-only samples. The results stem from an analysis of 47 studies conducted between 1982 and 2008. Even with mixed findings, and with the continuation of largely male-centered research in this area (Holtfreter & Cupp, 2007; Manchak et al., 2009; Hollin & Palmer, 2006), claims of gender-neutrality persist (Veysey & Hamilton, 2007).

Funk (1999) noted gender differences in an assessment instrument designed to predict the risk of re-offending. Funk tracked the juveniles in her study for two years and found that while the regression model predicting outcome for the entire sample and for the male-only sample were similar, the female-only model looked quite different. For females, person-related offenses, child abuse and/or neglect, and running away were significantly associated with reoffending. The adjusted R^2 for the female model was roughly twice that of the male-only model, suggesting that developing risk assessment instruments specifically with gender in mind will increase the predictive ability and validity of an instrument.

Harer and Langan (2001) found that the same classification instrument was able to predict violence equally well for male and female inmates. However, their analysis also demonstrates that women were significantly less likely than men to commit violent acts. Their study, then, begins to demonstrate the possibility that classification instruments may be able to predict similar behavior for men and women, but they do not account for the differences between them. It may be problematic to think of gender as just another predictor variable rather than to treat gender as a subset in which different variables pose a risk to re-offending.

Lowenkamp et al. (2001) found the LSI-R to be predictive of recidivism for both male and female offenders. Further, they discovered that past victimization did not enhance the predictive validity of the instrument. These authors argue that criminal thinking and attitude problems need to be addressed regardless of any history of past abuse. Yet, Benda later discovered the existence of a significant relationship between physical and sexual abuse (ever) and recidivism over a 5 year period. His sample utilized male and female boot camp graduates.

In a multivariate study of probationers, Olson et al. (2003) did find differences in predictors of recidivism (rearrest) for males and females. Using a sample of probationers in Illinois, they noted that men who recidivated were significantly more likely to be younger, single, gang members, high school dropouts, and have previous convictions and substance abuse problems. Female recidivists, on the other hand, exhibited low education and prior convictions as significant predictor variables. Being married did increase the odds of rearrest for females, but not significantly so; yet that being single for the males increased the odds of rearrest in this sample.

Holsinger et al. (2003) analyzed a sample of both male and female incarcerated and community-supervised offenders. While they did not examine outcome data, they did discover significant correlations between gender, ethnicity, and the LSI-R overall score; female scores were lower than male scores, similar to the 1996 Coulson et al. findings - 20.64 & 23.59, respectively. Although this allows for a determination of where differences exist for males and females, it is unknown why they in fact do exist for these assessments. For example, while Holsinger et al. (2003) found that females were more likely than males to rely on social assistance (a risk factor in the LSI-R), the quantitative analysis by Holtfreter et al. (2004) demonstrates that the overall poverty status of females, aside from mere reliance on social assistance, significantly predicted odds of recidivism. In fact, the LSI-R level of risk dropped out as a significant predictor of recidivism once poverty status was controlled. The difficulty with regard to generalizing the Holtfreter results, though, is that it is a female-only sample.

Hubbard & Pratt (2004) conducted a meta-analysis of studies that looked at predictors of delinquency for girls as compared to boys. They discovered the "same-different" phenomenon. In other words, many of the predictors of delinquency for boys were the same for girls, such as anti-social peers and behavior. However, other factors were predictive for girls and not for boys, such as school and family relationships and histories of abuse.

Reisig et al. (2006) also found a "same-different" phenomenon in the predictive validity of the LSI-R. The Reisig et al. study discovered that while predictive validity existed for women in their sample, the LSI-R was only predictive for women whose offending context paralleled that of male offenders. The LSI-R did not work well for socially and economically marginalized women who followed gendered pathways to offending. The exclusion of important predictors of (re)offending suggested by the pathways approach to female offending negatively impacted the utility of the instrument for this population.

Heilbrun et al. (2008) analyzed gender differences on select LSI-R domains for a group of offenders released to parole. These researchers discovered significant differences for male and females on the financial and companion domains. However, these results were not liked with outcome data.

Van Voorhis et al. (2008) discovered that the inclusion of gender-relevant factors proved to be better predictors of unwanted outcomes (institutional misconduct for prisoners and recidivism for community correctional populations) than were the so-called gender-neutral predictors of factors such as criminal history, antisocial associates, and substance abuse. These general findings stem from extensive research across various sites, including Hawai'i, and with samples of both institutional and community correctional populations.

Manchak et al. (2009) analyzed the predictive validity of a sample of 70 female and 1,035 male serious violent offenders. Their research discovered that the LSI-R worked well for women and, further, that gender did not moderate the prediction of recidivism via the LSI-R. They did notice domain differences by gender. The major flaw in this study is the small number of female offenders.

Most recently, Smith et al. (2009) ask us to consider whether claims of predictive validity based on 14,737 women can be wrong. The short answer is yes, they can. Smith et al. conducted a meta-analysis that included 25 studies of published LSI-R scores and outcomes. A total of 14,737 female offenders were thus included in this analysis. Their analysis demonstrated predictive validity for both males and females, yet the problem of a lack of gender-specific measures remains. Yet, this type of research fails to go beyond the overall outcome. If, for example, gender does not matter, why does some research demonstrate varied domain differences with outcome?

At face value, tools like the LSI-R appear to indeed be gender-neutral because *some* studies demonstrate predictive validity for both males and females (Raynor, 2007). Close scrutiny reveals that the research is not as clear. Important gender patterns do emerge when gender is analyzed separately, such as the importance of controlling for economic marginalization (Reisig et al., 2006) or other gender-specific factors (Van Voorhis et al., 2008). Thus, the results so far have not been uniform, indicating that gender matters in some respect (Manchak et al., 2009). It follows, then, that if gender does make a difference in the predictive validity of the LSI-R, then the failure to take these gender-specific factors into account is likely to harm or fail that population (e.g., females) whose factors have been largely ignored. Further, the lack of gender-specific variables involves two immediate difficulties for female offenders: issues of over- and/or under-classification, both of which pose harm to female offenders (Hubbard & Matthews, 2008).

Most notable in the literature is the issue of over-classification of women (Reisig et al., 2006; Blanchette & Brown, 2006; Holtfreter et al., 2004; Flavin, 2004; Austin, 2003; Bloom et al., 2003; Covington & Bloom, 2003; Farr, 2000; Olson et al., 2003; Brennan, 1998), yet this is an area also in need of more research (Hannah-Moffat & Shaw, 2003; Brennan, 1998). For example, if factors such as age and prior convictions are included as measures of risk, but are only statistically significant for men (Olson et al., 2003), then counting these same factors for women will effectively result in their over-classification. Austin notes that, for incarcerated populations, a failure to look at meaningful male/female differences in misconduct can result in over-classification of female offenders in an institutional setting. Over-classification can result in greater surveillance in the community or higher custody levels in institutional settings (Blanchette & Brown, 2006) than is actually warranted.

Under-classification could also occur because females, as compared to males, tend to commit less serious offenses, are less likely to use a weapon, and are less likely to have as lengthy a criminal history (Blanchette, 2004; James, 2004; Kruttschnitt and Gartner, 2003), and thus might inaccurately be scored as lower risk (Holtfreter & Cupp, 2007). If the qualitative differences that exist in terms of recidivism risk between men and women are not included in assessment instruments, then women's true risk will not be counted. This also becomes problematic when women are erroneously classified as low-risk and are hence not deemed appropriate targets for intervention (Reisig et al., 2006; Bloom et al., 2003). Whitaker (2000, pg. 5) notes, "Many women offenders supervised in the community are classified as low risk, and typically low risk offenders have little or no relationship with their agents. Because relationships are central to women's lives, it is predictable that women will experience a higher rate of failure on community supervision." Regardless of the scores in terms of the overall risk to recidivate, female offenders still have treatment needs that rival those of men (Blanchette, 2004). For example, James (2004) notes that females were significantly more likely (34.4%) than men (28.0%) to have used drugs at the time of their current offense, indicating a greater need for substance abuse treatment.

A survey of state practioners on the lack of gender-specific assessment instruments indicates a questioning of whether women are as dangerous as men and a "lack of attention to women's unique needs, criticizing classification models for their inattention to relationship, abuse, mental health, and parenting issues" (Van Voorhis & Presser, 2001). Latessa (1999) has noted the need to abandon a one-size fits all approach and that the examination of issues such as mental health, substance abuse, and criminal thinking may require many tools. And, as one of the creators of the LSI-R notes (Bonta et al., 1995), "The underrepresentation of women in conflict with the law has had an important impact on the services provided to female offenders and on theory development and research."

To reiterate, the lack of specific regard to variables that uniquely affect large numbers of female offenders has the possibility of creating over- or under-classification of these offenders. And, given that the LSI-R in Hawai'i, as elsewhere, will be used to route offenders into appropriate services, female offenders may consequently be over- or under-treated and supervised (Hannah-Moffat & Shaw, 2003). Furthermore, appropriate cutoff scores have not been developed for female-only samples, an area clearly in need of improvement (Hannah-Moffat & Shaw, 2003). At least one practitioner, Chia, (2000) notes that research efforts in her area have demonstrated the need for lower cutoff scores for female as compared to male offenders.

Recent literature, however, appears focused on the programming (to address criminogenic need factors) of women rather than on the classification (criminogenic risk factors) of women. As mentioned earlier, programmatic concerns, in Hawai'i anyway, will follow and not precede assessment, making this a timely issue for study. As such, it seems logical that the *context* of women's offending should be included in any attempt at an actuarial classification instrument[11]. The importance of a study such as this is implicated in a quote by McMahon (2000, pg. 298), "....women are recognized as low risk (and especially compared to the higher risk believed to be posed by men, following the actuarial approach would suggest that they be a low priority for receipt of services. In short, the traditional neglect of women within corrections seems to be reinforced by the actuarial approach."

Risk and need assessments may thus be the objective veil behind which we continue to ignore women in the criminal justice system. We need to move beyond predictive validity and also look at what these categories really mean and how well they work for treatment intervention (Manchak et al., 2009). Gender-responsive practices, ones that consider the context of female offender criminality, can improve outcomes. This approach is likely to prove more beneficial to both

---

[11] Hannah-Moffat and Shaw (2001) present a detailed list of studies that have documented the context within which women often commit offenses (15-16).

communities and female offenders (Bloom et al., 2003). In the area of risk assessment, which Harcourt (2007) terms more of an art than a science, it seems as if the weight of the gendered pathway literature, coupled with the ambiguity of empirical research on the most used risk/need instrument, the LSI-R, warrant a step in this direction.

Implications of the LSI-R for the Female Offender

It has been noted that, "A fair tool does not discriminate against offenders on the basis of enduring personal traits (e.g., race, gender, or age) and permits offenders equal access to services and treatment" (Holsinger et al., 2001, pg. 4). While this is a true statement, it becomes problematic when differential characteristics associated with populations who possess the above-mentioned enduring traits, such as women or minorities, are not considered prior to instrument construction. Otherwise, an implication is that these actuarial risk/need instruments are actually objective (and hence seemingly unbiased) means of delivering equal access to services and treatment. For the purposes of this research, the lack of regard to gender-specific risk/need items is especially problematic. It has recently been argued that the items that end up on a risk/need assessment instrument are there for one of two reasons: 1) they are based on a subjective assessment of professional judgment; or 2) empirical tests in which the analysis of large data sets dictate which items are probabilistically related to the criteria, or outcomes, of interest (Gottfredson & Snyder, 2005).

The problem, in the main, is that the female offender has been ignored on both accounts. Neither subjective knowledge of how female offending (pathways, current risks or needs) may differ from those of her male counterpart, nor the inclusion of women into original validation samples have been found in contemporary risk/need instruments. Rather, females are added to the equation only after one or both of the above-mentioned criteria have been met for men.

Regardless of an offender's placement in the criminal justice system (i.e., arrest, jail, probation, prison, parole, etc.), the population remains largely male. Yet, owing to continued growth of the correctional population, coupled with conservative social policies (including those associated with the war on drugs), the criminal justice population is increasingly likely to involve female offenders. The question here, then, is whether the newest generation of actuarial-based risk/need assessment instruments are valid on female offender populations, and, if so, whether predictive validity alone is enough to justify their use for female offenders (Maurutto & Hannah-Moffat, 2007).

Ultimately, the lack of a specific focus on females in this area of the criminal justice system poses serious potential problems for female offenders. Covington and Bloom (2003, pg. 9) provide a good summary of the issues involved:

> Valid and equitable classification is critical for women because it impacts decisions regarding programming, housing, work, and the perceptions of staff. The current "gender-neutral" classification systems, based on security and custody, incorrectly label and house women at higher levels than necessary. Actuarial tools are used to classify prisoners in terms of security risks as well as in terms of criminogenic needs.

Although Covington and Bloom are discussing issues dealing with institutional classification, parallel problems and concerns are also raised when the focus shifts to community correctional populations. In the end, it is important to consider the important context of female offending. Unfortunately current risk/need instruments, such as the LSI-R, currently fail to capture context (Hubbard & Matthews, 2008).

Once a criminogenic risk or need has been identified, it must be dealt with (Loader & Sparks, 2002). So, once a jurisdiction makes the decision to utilize a risk/need based actuarial instrument, some potential outcome of assessment must be managed. As stated in Loader & Sparks, this means that as agencies embrace more of the risk terminology, they must also spend more time 'monitoring, adjusting, and calculating' their practices and behaviors in light of the outcome that the instrument was intended to deal with.

Hawai'i's correctional system has decided to use the LSI-R as the risk assessment of choice. In Hawai'i, correctional stakeholders hope to accomplish a 30% percent reduction in recidivism through the best risk/need assessment and treatment/intervention process possible. High risk offenders are prioritized for treatment under the assumption that treatment of the highest risk offenders will yield the greatest reduction in recidivism. This is the so-called risk principle (Van Voorhis, 2005). It is theorized that appropriate offender assessments will help direct resources to those most at risk (Bonta et al., 2001; Smith et al., 2009). Further, there is an existing literature which demonstrates that providing intensive intervention/treatment services to low risk offenders actually serves to *increase* recidivism (Andrews et al., 1989, Bonta, 1996). Thus, higher risk offenders receive more and better services and a higher level of supervision, while lower risk offenders receive less service and supervision.

The Hawai'i version of Intermediate Sanctions, coupled with the use of the LSI-R, is to triage the highest risk offenders into treatment, or more intensive treatment, with lower risk offenders receiving less treatment, or no treatment at all. Yet the presence of a larger population of male offenders drives the average for all offenders. And, since males are more likely to score higher than females, there will necessarily be a higher risk cutoff for all offenders. Women will be shortchanged under the guise of an objective instrument that qualifies both supervision and treatment. As a result, under-classification could be just as harmful to the female offender as over-classification. It is important to note that, in a meta-analysis, Dowden and Andrews (1999) found that the treatment principles tied to instruments such as the LSI-R are effective at reducing female recidivism. However, if the different factors that are related to female offending are not accounted for at the onset, then effective interventions for women will be missed.

The approach currently implemented in Hawai'i is one based on cognitive restructuring and relies, in part, on strategies of responsivity. This means that an offenders' treatment is matched with his/her learning style. Additionally, the stress on creating relationships with the client may indicate, given that females are much more likely than males to be relationship oriented (Hannah-Moffat & Shaw, 2001), a better conduit for care than that which previously exists. Counter to any notion of a new penological method of community supervision, then, Hawai'i remains committed to offender change. However, there may be, in reality, difficulty fully implementing this method of offender supervision at the front line level (Lynch, 1998).

Conclusion

The research that will be presented here is particularly timely in Hawai'i, since Hawai'i, as other states, will be assessing men and women under the assumption that they are, from a risk to re-offend standpoint, the same. However, the validity of the LSI-R in recidivism prediction for women is clearly in question. We need to make sure that we have a link between criminology and the criminal justice system and its associated practices. These two areas should inform and influence one another.

Key issues exist with regard to the use of actuarial risk/need instruments, such as the LSI-R, on female offender populations. To reiterate, it is important that work on the prediction of criterion variables be "applied to groups of persons who are similar in terms of some set of characteristics, rather than to individuals" (Gottfredson & Snyder, 2005, Pg. 7). If we believe that female offenders are, on the whole, significantly different than male offenders, then risk/need assessment instruments derived from male samples are rendered problematic.

Although this research investigates whether or not the LSI-R is equitable in terms of predictive and content validity for female versus male offenders, the point is not lost that even this exercise is problematic given the statement above. While validations should be attempted on populations other than those on which the original instrument was created, a validation of this instrument on female offenders may not actually mean that it is a fair instrument because of the theoretical discounting of female specific factors – the built in neglect of gender. Indeed, Gottfredson & Snyder (2005) suggest that one method of improving such instruments is via the collection of data that have a hypothesized relation to the criterion (for the purpose of this research, the criterion is recidivism). In the case of the LSI-R, this was not done. Rather, the LSI-R and similar instruments assume objectivity in measurement across gender, yet this may very well be a flawed assumption (Maurutto & Hannah-Moffat, 2007; Holtfreter & Cupp, 2007; Blanchette & Brown, 2006). As Harcourt (2007) notes, the debate over the use of actuarial instruments is one, "about mathematics, identifiable social costs, and epistemic distortions." Importantly, too, is the recognition that similar predictive ability and common risks/needs for males and females does not mean they are *experienced* in the same manner (Hollin & Palmer, 2006).

This chapter demonstrates the need for a link between theories of female offending with the current application (and creation) of actuarial based risk/need instruments. Current instruments have so far failed to do so. It is important to investigate the predictive and content validity of these instruments. The next chapter discusses some of the methodological concerns from a feminist methodology perspective as well as why it is important to push beyond the traditional predictive validity approach in the validation of these instruments. Rather, the argument is made that we should also include a more qualitative approach to ensure we measure content validity. It is the latter area that currently calls for greater research attention and scrutiny.

CHAPTER 3

Making Gender Count: Measuring the Impact of Gender on Risk & Need Instruments

I understand gender to be far more than the simple dichotomy of male and female. Gender is a whole set of social relations that organize us into different social positions with different advantages and constraints based on our sexual preferences and our parental status.
-Joey Sprague

Every con has a story to tell.
-Parolee on willingness to talk to researchers.

Introduction

The impact of gender in criminological research is historically complicated by a gender ratio problem and a larger generalizability problem (Hannah-Moffat, 2009; Daly & Chesney-Lind, 1988). Criminologists, in the main, have tended to 'add gender and stir' with regard to the study of myriad criminological problems. Indeed, a major critique of what we "know" in criminology is what we actually know about male-centered criminology (Chesney-Lind, 2006; Miller, 2005). We understand a lot about male crime initiation, criminal careers, and desistance but relatively little about these same issues for female offenders (Chesney-Lind, 2006; Sommers et al., 2006).

The study of actuarial risk/need assessment instruments has been no different in this regard, save a handful of studies. As outlined in the previous chapter, these instruments have been built around theory and knowledge of male offenders and merely applied to female offenders. This unfortunately begs the question of whether any significantly predictive relationships are indeed genuine or, rather, are spurious in nature.

This research stems from a concern about the manner in which gender really counts in risk/need assessment instruments. Specifically, the concern is whether past methods have helped maintain a male-based status quo and, ultimately, undermined the notion of equality and justice for female offenders (Sprague, 2005). In order to adequately address this issue, one must begin with gender in mind (Taylor & Blanchette, 2009).

This study is certainly timely. The LSI-R is the most widely used risk/need assessment instrument in the United States and has been readily adopted in many other countries as well (Smith et al., 2009; Lowenkamp & Latessa, 2004b; Manchak et al., 2009). However, there is still a paucity of research regarding the appropriateness and usefulness of this and similar actuarial based risk/need instruments for female offenders. And, as outlined in the first chapter of this book, this fact is further complicated by the rate of growth in the female correctional population – a rate that has outpaced male offenders for the past decade. Unfortunately, many jurisdictions have adopted these types of instruments wholesale without any validation on their offender populations, including by gender (Brumbaugh et al., 2005). This chapter addresses the importance of utilizing feminist methods generally and with respect to risk/need instruments specifically. A review of the explicit research questions is also included, along with the methods and samples used in this study.

Counting Within a Feminist Framework

There really is not one accepted feminist method for quantitative or qualitative researchers. Indeed, research methods per se are generally standard across disciplines, and technically this is the same regarding feminist methods. The conceptual framework of a study is what marks feminist methods from mainstream methods. The feminist standpoint is typically motivated from the historical exclusion of women and girls in criminological research and the development of knowledge based on male only samples. These traditional methods have merely assumed gender neutrality.

As such, many feminists argue for gender-centered research. For researchers working from a feminist standpoint, this means making women the center of inquiry. Scholarship via a feminist lens asks us to thoughtfully question taken-for-granted assumptions regarding traditional research practices and to understand that knowledge is a by-product of socially dominant relationships (e.g., patriarchy) (Sprague, 2005). One of the ways that feminist researchers make certain that gendered knowledge can emerge is to ensure that women's voices are heard as part of the research process (Belknap, 2007).

Further, many feminist researchers argue that the best way to study a social problem is via a multiple method approach, especially one that merges quantitative and qualitative modes of data collection (Holtfreter & Cupp, 2007). We often neglect the use of multiple methods in criminological research. Indeed, the most valid research outcomes often necessitate multiple methodologies. For example, in the documentation of how the context of female domestic violence arrests are masked by sheer quantitative data alone, Miller (2005) reminds us that multiple methods are important in the evaluation of multiple perspectives. Miller discovered that quantitative data on domestic violence arrests were misleading in light of the actual context of the problem. While women's arrests for domestic violence have increased, largely owing to legal changes, Miller demonstrates that the reasons for and the actual manner in which women commit violence is qualitatively different from men.

This is emblematic of the contradiction between the quantitative (e.g., women are violent too, just look at the numbers) versus the qualitative (e.g., women's violence is often a direct response to their subordinate positions in intimate relationships). In other words, Miller's work demonstrates that violence committed by women, in the main, is contextually different. These important patterns only emerged through her use of multiple methods. While our field has certainly favored quantitative data collection and analysis as ideal, the neglect of a gendered lens in these types of studies has also shielded us from necessarily collecting or counting all data that are important to female offenders (Belknap, 2007). The inclusion of qualitative methods, and offender voice, informs us about the types of questions or variables we should quantitatively count (Belknap, 2007), the standpoint of those under study (Morash, 2009), and whether you can adequately measure certain concepts out of context (Sprague, 2005). Sprague (2005, pg. 84) importantly notes the implications of this traditional neglect:

Every measurement approach creates a pattern of selective visibility: it taps some aspects of a phenomenon and hides others. Measures are always constructed within specific historical and political contexts that shape what is measured and how. Mainstream practices put researchers in control of what an idea means, how to word questions, and what will be on the menu of legitimate responses. Whether researchers write their own measures or use measures that that have been used in other studies, the selection favors the standpoint of researchers, particularly the most prolific and/or prominent researchers.....and this tends to be a fairly homogenous and privileged group.

This study stems from a related concern and adopts a similar perspective via a questioning of whether the generally accepted knowledge base for risk/need instruments is indeed generalizeable to women in the first place. The framework for questioning the appropriateness of male-based instruments for female offenders begins from a pathways perspective, as noted in Chapter 1. It is important to mention that Bloom et al. (2003) note that the pathways perspective supports multiple methods, ones that of necessity include females at the fore. Indeed, it is worth noting that researchers have discovered important differences in how the LSI-R, in particular, operates after utilizing samples of representative female offenders who followed specific gendered pathways to offending (Holtfreter & Cupp, 2007).

However, it is important that feminist criminology not forget about the boys in the same manner that mainstream criminology has forgotten about the girls. Even at those times when the traditional neglect of the female offender has come to the forefront, it has often been at the abandon of including *both* males and females together (Benda, 2005) for important comparative analyses (Belknap & Holsinger, 2006). Feminist criminology must also not make the mistake of only theorizing and studying girls and women. While the previous section mentioned the need to place girls and women at the center of research, a decidedly gendered center should be the framework that guides analyses (Chesney-Lind, 2006) that, ideally, will involve both girls and boys so that appropriate comparisons can be made (Belknap & Holsinger, 2006; Benda, 2005).

Gendered Risk & Need Research: Gaining Momentum

The overwhelming focus of study in the area of risk/need instruments has been on testing the predictive validity of these instruments generally and, to a lesser extent but increasingly so, on female offenders (Holtfreter & Cupp, 2007). As has been argued elsewhere, studies that rely on male only samples or that simply use gender as a control variable call into question the applicability to female offenders (Belknap, 2007). Indeed, Holtfreter & Cupp (2007) note that only 11 of 41 studies published from 1998 through 2006 that dealt with the LSI/ LSI-R reported statistics on females. This amounts to roughly one-quarter of the work through 2006. While this area of criminological study has certainly gained momentum in recent years, there is clearly a documented need for continued improvement.

However, the increased amount of studies does not resolve the methodological issues with many 'gendered' studies that do exist in this area. Researchers have generally adopted one of two methods when it comes to a specific gendered approach to the study of risk/need instruments: (1) the 'add gender and stir' method and (2) these use of female only samples.

This first method - 'add gender and stir' – includes those studies that typically employ gender only as a variable. In other words, male and female samples are used to test these instruments, but the analyses are not segregated by gender. Instead, aggregate models are used and gender is merely controlled for. The results stemming from these types of methods are popular in criminology to assure us that gender does not matter - or, often using sophisticated statistical modeling with gender as a dummy variable, how gender does matter.

However, there are problems with this approach. Namely, and often owing to the larger number of males relative to females, correlations become inflated or are otherwise misleading because any significant findings tend to be skewed by the larger number of male offenders in a sample relative to the females and, too, may ultimately yield unanticipated social and economic costs (Holtfreter & Cupp, 2007). When we do discover statistically significant findings we assume them to be substantive for all under study (Sprague, 2005). We simply lose the importance of female only significant factors or differences between the females and males (Hannah-Moffat, 2009; Sprague, 2005).

The second manner of assessing the utility of these instruments is to pull samples of only female offenders and then analyze female offenders alone. This is certainly an improvement over the gender as a variable approach (Sprague, 2005). Specifically, this method is argued to enhance the ability of the context of female offending to emerge (Holtfreter & Cupp, 2007; Reisig et al., 2006).

However, the desire at the end is to then ask, "Compared to what?" A strength, it seems, is to pull samples of both male and female offenders who are similarly situated in the system and then compare the results of male- and female-only models. For example, in an analysis of a risk/need instrument, Funk (1999) discovered that the results of a predictive validity test for the male-only model were similar to those produced by the mixed gender model. The female only model demonstrated significantly different patterns, ones in which child abuse/neglect and running away were able to emerge as predictive of re-offending for the girls. Importantly, Funk (1999) also discovered that the combined model explained less variance than the gendered model. Veysey & Hamilton (2007) also discovered both different variables and different strengths in correlation with recidivism for single-gender models versus combined gender models where sex was merely a control variable.

Of course, the argument can also be made that we need not test these types of instruments on females at all. Rather, we should construct gender-responsive risk/need instruments from the ground up (Taylor & Blanchette, 2009; Hannah-Moffat, 2009; Veysey & Hamilton, 2007). Baird (2009) poses this relevant question regarding risk/need assessment instruments, "Can the inclusion of factors without significant statistical relationships to recidivism actually *reduce*, rather than improve, a model's ability to accurately classify cases?" (emphasis in original). This is essentially the possible danger of the 'add gender and stir' method and the need for specifically gendered models. We will certainly return to this issue at the end of this book. For now, though, it is important to critically assess the importance of methodology and the impact on findings.

There seem to be two primary areas of neglect thus far. First, while it is instructive and an improvement to analyze female only samples and models, the comparison with similarly situated male offenders is lost. Second, the primary focus on the quantitative continues to hide a larger issue of content validity and whether, as with Miller's (2005) research, the numbers hide the context and other qualitative differences that might exist between male and female offenders (Hannah-Moffat, 2009; Sprague, 2005).

It seems transparent that one should also be concerned with content validity if the context of the items measured on risk/need assessment instruments is indeed gendered. Generally speaking, content validity refers to (Singleton et al., 1993), "the extent to which a measure adequately represents all facets of a concept." Yet, content validity has been ignored because academics and practioners working in this field have merely assumed that female offenders are the same as male offenders and, thus, the content of these instruments applies equally. This research tests and challenges that assumption. It is of paramount importance to discover the manner in which content validity may differ for female and male offenders, although most jurisdictions have failed to take on this task (Taylor & Blanchette, 2009; Hannah-Moffat, 2009; Sprague, 2005). With specific regard to the LSI-R, we should be concerned with whether or not the domains captured in the LSI-R assessment actually tap into all relevant components of that domain.

Framework for the Current Study

In an effort to improve upon past methods of gendered risk/need instrument studies, the current study employees multiple methods. Female offenders were a primary consideration in the organizing framework for this study from the beginning. To reiterate, this research seeks to address two primary research questions: (1) Is the Level of Service Inventory – Revised (LSI-R), which was created for and heavily validated on a male offender population, valid in the prediction of criminal recidivism for female offenders? (2) Does the LSI-R demonstrate content validity for both male and female offenders?

The 'Traditional Predictive' Validity Approach

The answer to the predictive validity question inevitably requires a quantitative analysis. This investigation requires the traditional test of whether the instrument in question is able to accurately predict what it purports to predict – in this case recidivism. As the next chapter will demonstrate, descriptive statistics and multivariate analyses were utilized to assess differences in the LSI-R scores for men and women, domain scores, and, ultimately, the ability of the instrument to predict recidivism for both male and female offenders. Analyses were run for the entire combined sample and by gender.

This portion of the study involved the analysis of existing data. Data collected as part of an on-going study of recidivism in the State of Hawai`i were utilized to discern whether the LSI-R, currently in use in Hawai`i, demonstrated gender-specific differences in overall scores, domain scores, and recidivism. This predictive validity approach is a largely inductive one since, based on the existing literature, one should expect there to be meaningful differences between the levels of risk, overall and by domains, between men and women. Importantly, this study contributes to a paucity of research on the gendered nature of actuarial risk/need instruments (Funk, 1999; Brennan, 1998; Bonta & Motiuk, 1992) via the specific inclusion of women in the analyses, building upon studies that have already included males, especially young males, and certain ethnic groups, such as Native American males.

Participants for this portion of the study included all parolees and felony probationers who were released to community supervision via parole or sentenced to felony probation in the State of Hawai`i between January 23, 1998 and February 1, 2005. The variation in these dates certainly requires some explanation. Having received an LSI-R assessment was the starting point for creating this database. All offenders in the State of Hawai`i who had an LSI-R assessment *and* who had at least a year of exposure in the community were included in this study. Statewide use of the LSI-R in Hawai`i began in 2001, but there were a few cases assessed prior to that time. Offenders were tracked from the time of release or sentence to community supervision through February 1, 2006. This time frame ensured that each offender had at least one year of exposure in the community. Although longer follow-up times are preferred, one year is adequate given that given a majority (over two-thirds) of offenders who will recidivate do so within the first year of exposure (Langan & Levin, 2002; Manchak et al., 2009; Deschenes et al., 2006).

Drawing on the earlier discussion of the need to include studies that look at both similarly situated males and females, with significant female offender sample sizes, it is noteworthy that this sample included 462 women and 2,046 men (see Table 3.1), a relatively large female offender sample size for this type of research (Holtfreter & Cupp,

2007). Again, past research of this type has included smaller female sample sizes which have hindered both analyses and results (Hubbard & Matthews, 2008; Manchak et al., 2009; Olson et al., 2003; Fagan et al., 2007). Additionally, the sample is taken from the same cohort of offenders, thereby avoiding the pitfalls of some previous research that made comparisons between randomly selected male samples and conveniently selected female samples (Hannah-Moffat & Shaw, 2003; Holtfreter & Cupp, 2007; Taylor & Blanchette, 2009).

The sample utilized for this predictive validity study does have limitations that are necessary to point out. The overall representativeness of *all* male and female offenders is not maintained in this sample. The State of Hawai`i uses a pre-screening instrument prior to the application of the LSI-R. This screen, termed the proxy, is used to ensure that the LSI-R is applied only to the riskiest population of offenders. The proxy is a screening instrument comprised of three items, including age at first arrest, number of prior arrests, and current age. The answers to these questions are weighted whereby higher scoring offenders go forth to receive an LSI-R assessment while lower scoring offenders do not.

Some might ask why all offenders are not subject to this LSI-R assessment. Readers familiar with the state of caseloads on probation and parole already know the answer to this question. Given the high caseloads in Hawai`i, as with most jurisdictions, there is a desire to target, in the most meaningful ways, the highest risk offenders. As such, a decision was made at the onset of the LSI-R adoption in Hawai`i to assess only the riskiest 55% of the overall offender population with the remaining 45% to be supervised at a much lower level of surveillance and without the aid of a risk/need instrument.

Recidivism is generally the primary outcome of interest in risk/need instrument prediction research. Recidivism can and has been measured in myriad ways. In this study, though, recidivism is conceptualized as a new felony arrest or revocation of community status while on felony probation or parole. This measure was dichotomized and coded as either "0" for no recidivism, or "1" indicating an episode of recidivism.

Table 3.1 Quantitative Sample Description: Total, Male, and Female Sample

	Total (n=2,508)	Male (n=2,046)	Female (n=462)
	Percents		
Supervising agency			
Probation	89.9	89.6	91.1
Parole	10.1	10.4	8.9
Average age	31.7	32.0	30.6
Marital Status			
Divorced	12.1	11.6	14.1
Married	12.4	12.2	13.4
Separated	4.0	3.9	4.5
Single, never-married	70.6	71.7	66.0
Widowed	0.8	0.6	1.9
Ethnicity			
Hawaiian/part-Hawaiian	43.6	42.7	47.6
Caucasian	16.4	15.9	18.3
Filipino	8.4	8.9	5.9
Japanese	3.0	2.9	3.0
Pacific Islander	8.3	8.6	6.9
Black	2.5	2.7	1.6
Other Asian	2.5	2.6	2.1
Hispanic	2.7	3.0	1.6
Other	12.7	12.6	13.0
Current Offense			
Person	28.9	32.6	13.0
Property	31.6	29.8	39.8
Drugs	18.5	17.2	24.5
Other	20.9	20.5	22.7

The independent, or predictor, variables include the following: 1) demographics, including gender, age, and ethnicity; (2) total LSI-R scores, obtained through the parole and probation officer's assessments; 3) domain scores within the LSI-R, obtained through the parole and probation officer's assessments (e.g., criminal history, education & employment, financial, family & marital, accommodation, leisure & recreation, companions, alcohol & drug, emotional & personal, and attitudes & orientation); 4) the current, or most serious offense for which the offender was sentenced, or released, to community supervision; and 5) type of community supervision (i.e., parole or felony probation). The primary predictors, as presented in Chapter 4, are the total LSI-R scores and the domain subscale scores (run separately due to multicolinearity).

Although other analyses may be of greater sociological interest to some readers, a critique of various types of advanced statistical modeling has been wisely noted (Geortzel, 2002). It is therefore important in this study that the test of predictive validity be centered on the actual use of this instrument. Ultimately, we want to know whether our statistical models here, much like the actuarial risk/need instrument, is able to make predictions of recidivism better than random chance alone (Geortzel, 2002).

As demonstrated in the next Chapter, overall scores, domain scores, and individual factors were compared first using descriptive statistics. Inter-gender differences were detected via the use of t-tests for difference in means and chi-square tests for gender differences. Pearson's r statistics were utilized to determine the correlation of total and domain scores with recidivism.

A multivariate statistical technique known as survival analysis is utilized to test the predictive validity of the instrument. Survival analysis is well suited for event history analyses, which describes a family of statistical procedures that measure time from a starting date (e.g., the start of community supervision) to a termination date (e.g., an episode of recidivism) within a specified period of observation. This method of analysis also controls for each offender's time at risk, which is especially important since each offender will have varying exposure times. Cox regression is the specific method of survival analysis employed for this study. Additionally, and unlike traditional forms of multivariate regression, Cox regression allows the dependent variable to be dichotomized (e.g., a recidivating event versus no recidivating event). The results of this traditional predictive validity test are presented in the next chapter.

The Interviews & Content Validity

There are multiple measures of validity, one of which is predictive validity, but another important measure is content validity. This is an area largely unexplored in the literature as it relates to actuarial risk/need instruments. Assessing whether risk *means* the same thing for men and women requires a qualitative methodology. Specifically, male and female offenders who were under community correctional supervision (e.g., felony probation or parole) were interviewed to assess the risks for recidivism in their lives – from their perspective. Sprague (2005) reminds us that by listening to groups who have been traditionally neglected in research (e.g., female offenders) we create enormous opportunities to uncover what quantitative analyses might have otherwise been obscured. Interview methodologies thus allow us to, "document the lives and activities of women, understand the experience of women from their own point of view, and conceptualize women's behavior as an expression of social contexts" (Owen, 1998).

The predictive validity component of this research is timely and practical, but it is also important to note that (Van Voorhis, 2005), "...it's not entirely about prediction. It's about whether we could have a better instrument for women if we developed a separate system with women in mind. It's about understanding how risk factors may be interpreted differently for men and women." Others have also voiced the need to look at content validity as different from predictive validity (Hannah-Moffat &Shaw, 2003) and the need to focus on gendered variation in the context and content of re-offending. This portion of the research thus employs a grounded theory approach to data collection. The intent was to listen to what both the men and the women had to say about their life histories and the factors that they felt put them at risk for re-offending (Gilfus, 2006). A dual purpose of the interviews with offenders, therefore, was to build a base of comparison between female and male offenders, as well as to inform the quantitative portion of the study. In other words, is there universal content validity in what the LSI-R questions measure, or is it really a means of objectively scoring male-defined responses? Further, does risk and need *mean* the same thing for males and females?

Although it is certainly expected that males and females will give varied answers to common questions, the actual substance and degree of difference in their answers is nonetheless speculative. Yet, assessing ideas about risk/need from the offender's point of view is important because the quantitative portion of the analysis would not fully explicate whether there was content validity in what is being predicted (or predicting what we think we are predicting) versus what it is about the risk/need items being measured themselves, beyond mere statistical quantification (Gilfus, 2006).

It is through the qualitative research approach that one is able to gain a fuller understanding of the problem under exploration, and giving the people under study a voice is one method of facilitating this process. For example, Bloom et al. (pg. 52, 2003) note that, "the pathways research has used extensive interviews with women to uncover the life events that place girls and women at risk of offending." Ultimately, allowing both women (Comack, 2006) and men to voice their own stories, in their own narratives, allows for greater understanding of the complexity of life trajectories with past, current, and future offending.

This research sought to make a logical continuance of this research path and utilizes face-to-face interviews to uncover events that female and male offenders believe put them at risk for re-offending. The distinction is that this research is not primarily focused on initial offending. Rather, the focus is on risks and needs present at the time of community supervision. Others have discovered that when offenders are allowed to use their own voice, they are able to clearly delineate an understanding of how their past lives 'caused' their criminal offending (Gilfus, 2006; Belknap & Holsinger, 2006).

As noted elsewhere, important decisions regarding supervision and interventions are becoming increasingly dependent on the basis of actuarial instruments, such as the LSI-R. Clear (pg. 213, 2003) states, "the validity of the technical base of a correctional classification process is important because it affects liberty and the experience of the penalty in so many ways." Conducting interviews with the offenders themselves helps to get at the content validity questions that are so important to this population (Hannah-Moffat & Shaw 2001). For example, is a need or risk as defined by the LSI-R *really* a need or risk for these women, in the same way as it is for the men? Bloom et al.

(2003) note (citing Van Voorhis) that exact terms, such as high risk or anti-social peers, have different meanings for men and women. Austin (2003) further explains that while a risk factor may pass the face validity test it may not pass the predictive test, and vice versa. Severson and Duclos (2005), for example, discovered the necessity of incorporating culture into correctional assessment instruments in their research of a suicide screening instrument for Native Americans. This was discovered only through interviewing the inmates rather than going through a standard assessment protocol.

Jones (pg. 64, 1994) noted that, "All prediction instruments inevitably reflect the behavior not only of the people studied but also of the people who created the instruments." This poignant statement becomes especially important regarding female offenders since the framers of most third-generation risk/need instruments, including the LSI-R, did not include theories of female offending. Jones further notes that, "Theory rather than data availability should drive the initial identification of possible predictor variables." While the LSI-R is built around theory, the theoretical base is still a male-centered one. It is incumbent upon contemporary research to attempt to broaden the focus of information and correlates of recidivism for women and determine how these may fit into risk/need instruments. Additionally, oftentimes the information theorized or otherwise predicted to be correlated with female recidivism is not systematically collected (Funk, 1999), increasing the need to look for alternate sources of data regarding gender and risk.

Interviewing offenders might also raise important questions that would otherwise be missed in a purely quantitative context (Richards & Ross, 2003). Petersilia (2003), for example, notes that the correlation between LSI-R scores and recidivism is 0.35. This figure might be increased with greater knowledge, from inmate voice rather than inmate files, which are largely compiled and studied void offender voice. Finally, Gilfus (2006) points out that:

> While in recent years there has been a burst of scholarly attention to women and crime, very few studies have been based on data obtained first hand from the women themselves in order to explore their own perceptions, and motivations for engaging in illegal activity. Nor have any studies focused specifically on women's criminal careers, how women enter

into illegal activities, and what kind of progression occurs over time.

In order to get a better understanding of the meaning of risk/need (and, as by-products, criminal careers and desistance), interviews were conducted with female and male felony probationers and parolees in Hawai`i. Although the focus of this research is clearly female in nature, the inclusion of males in the interview sample creates an important comparison group for the females. Otherwise, it is impossible to state with any certainty that the answers given by the females are any different than those that might have been provided by the males. There is much to be gained by talking to offenders about their perceptions of risk and the potential causes of those risks (Belknap & Holsinger, 2001). Following this, 31 individuals serving time on either parole or felony probation were interviewed for this study, including 13 females and 18 males. These interview data are instrumental in understanding pathways, criminal careers, desistance, and risk for recidivism as these factors have meaning in the context of their daily lives. It should be noted, though, that these qualitative results are exploratory. Yet, the intention is nonetheless to move risk/need assessment forward via a greater understanding of the content of these risk/need items so routinely and 'objectively' scored.

The sample for the qualitative analysis was not as easily obtained as was the quantitative data sample. The target was still parolees and felony probationers in Hawai`i. Recruitment of the interview sample involved two sites – the Hawai`i Paroling Authority, located in downtown Honolulu, and the Adult Probation Division of the State Judiciary, First Circuit Court, also located in downtown Honolulu. The formal method of recruitment for each agency follows:

1. Hawai`i Paroling Authority[12]: A flyer with my name, phone number, and departmental affiliation with the University of

---

[12] A concerted effort was made to exclude mentally ill and sex offender parolees from this sample. While I had no control over who would actually pick up a flyer and respond to my offer of an interview and incentive, I did not leave flyers at the Special Services Parole Office in Hawai`i. This office handles most of the mentally ill and sex offender parolees.

Hawai'i[13] was given to parole supervisors and administrators. Copies were also placed at the HPA front office in a place easily viewed by parolees as they checked in for their respective office appointments. Some parole officers also kept flyers at their desks and were instructed to tell the parolees that the decision to participate was completely theirs, and that their decision would neither negatively nor positively affect their parole status. In addition, it is important that parole officers instructed parolees that their participation or non-participation was completely voluntary, and the only person who would know about such participation would be the researcher. Recruitment was done in waves until the total sample size was met. Basically, a non-probability quota sampling method was utilized. The flyers to the parolees instructed them to contact me directly if they were interested in participating in the research. Incentives were offered for participation ($35 gift card for Long's Drug Store), with instructions that the parolee could withdraw or refuse any questions at any time.

2. State of Hawai'i Judiciary, Adult Probation Division: A flyer with my name, phone number, and departmental affiliation with the University of Hawai'i was given to the Adult Probation Administrator for Oahu. The administrator placed flyers in the waiting area where probationers could easily view them as they checked in for their respective office appointments. As with parole, recruitment was done in waves until the total sample size was met. Basically, a non-probability quota sampling method was utilized. The flyers to the probationers instructed them to contact me directly if they were interested in participating in the research. Incentives were offered for participation ($35 gift card for Long's Drug Store), with instructions that the probationer could withdraw or refuse any questions at any time.

It is worth noting some of the methodological difficulties associated with attempting to interview a group of offenders who are on felony probation or on parole. This is a sample that is difficult to 'get at.' I had

---

[13] These interviews were conducted while I was a PhD candidate at the University of Hawai'i at Manoa.

Making Gender Count

anticipated that offering a $25[14] gift card for a two-hour interview would rather quickly draw a sample of 50 interviewees. However, I experienced several difficulties in attempting to work with this population. First, not nearly as many parolees or probationers responded to my solicitation as I might have expected. Indeed, for every stack of 50 flyers left at a particular site (either probation or parole) I received, on average, about 7 contact cards.

Although this sounds somewhat promising, this led to two related problems. First, I called those who expressed interest to set up interviews. We would usually agree on a date, time, and place for the interview – almost always in a public setting. However, what often occurred was that I would arrive at the designated place, at the designated time, on the designated day, but the intended interviewee would not appear. Even with one or two reschedules, some just never appeared. This proved very frustrating. In fact, at one point I humorously considered skipping straight to a policy recommendation that included giving all individuals on parole and probation watches and calendars, and training them on their use. There were days in which I was convinced that this was really all this population needed to reduce recidivism.

A related concern came with non-returned calls. This was, ultimately, a more prevalent, yet less time-consuming problem. Many parolees and probationers took the time to send in a post card with their name and phone numbers listed (an indication of interest in this study). Yet, when I called them to set up an interview, they did not return my phone calls. I typically did not call more than three times. Part of the issue became one of personal discomfort – I began to feel as though I needed to play the role of a stereotypical 'used car salesman' if I wanted to get these individuals to meet with me.

These were not necessarily unexpected outcomes, though. Sprague (2005) discusses the issues of poor individuals having competing demands on both their time and energy and, as such, they are often 'no shows' on interview appointments. Sprague cites that there are often good intentions by the subjects, or potential subjects, on the day they agree to participate. However, it may be that when the time comes to

---

[14] This is similar to the incentive value given in other similarly-focused research (Reisig et al., 2006).

make an interview appointment, more pressing concerns in their daily lives demand attention over and above an interview (Sprague, 2005).

I did ultimately manage to obtain a sufficient number of interviews for the purposes of this study (though stopped short of my original quota. Although I offered an incentive for participation – a $35 gift card to Long's Drug Store (increased from an original $25 amount in order to increase participation) – I certainly always felt like I was cheating these men and women who were serving time on parole and probation. They all had such rich histories to tell and experiences to share. Often, their stories were such that they could make the toughest among us cry. But some also revealed current ongoing illegal activities (continued crime and drug use) – they shared this at great potential risk to themselves. I was asking them to share all of this with me, for a mere $35 to spend at Long's. The depth of their sharing was immense, and I always felt a little cheaper for having engaged in this. This feeling was certainly exacerbated with the knowledge that there tended to be both a class and a race differential between myself and the subjects of these interviews. Part of the personal discomfort, then, stemmed from realizing that there was a significant difference in social capital between myself, an educated white woman not in the criminal justice system, and these often marginalized men and women who were in the criminal justice system. Further, some of these individuals were triply marginalized via their status as poor, minority, women - aside from being in the correctional system.

Regardless, this type of interview process – hearing from both the female and male offenders – is an area often neglected in criminological research and, thus, well worth any discomfort I may have experienced. I also often felt that most of those who were being interviewed appreciated the chance to be heard in a non-judgmental manner. I was, after all, there to learn *from* them. I suspect that for most of those in my sample, this is a foreign concept.

The interviews themselves were typically conducted in public places that were semi-private (e.g., the YWCA, Starbucks, parks). Interviews lasted anywhere from an hour to over six for one. The average interview was a little over two hours. This duration is consistent with other researchers gathering life history data from female offenders or female inmates (Gilfus, 2006; Reisig et al., 2006; Sommers et al., 2006), and speaks to the rapport that was ultimately able to develop, aside from the social distance between the researched and the researcher.

I think that, for the parolees and probationers who took the time to talk with me, there was a general willingness to open up and share. As the opening quote for this chapter suggests, many of the men and women who have been involved in the criminal justice system truly do want to talk. They do not, however, want to be punished for doing so. For example, MJ, one of the male parolees I interviewed, clearly expressed a desire to share everything, but wanted reassurances that no one from parole would find out what he had said to me. Sal, another parolee, shared his hesitation to participate in this study as a trust issue. He had participated in an earlier research project while he was an inmate in a mainland prison and was assured anonymity. However, he stated that a report was later released with his name & CDC number alongside his personal quotes.

Finally, some offenders have been 'set-up' in undercover stings and are acutely cautious of these interview techniques. For example, Kaimi was set up by a trusted client who had secretly taped a drug transaction as a 'snitch' for the police. He was very uneasy about having our interview taped. It is interesting that the trust and sharing issues mainly came from the males in this sample. The female interviewees did not demonstrate the same level of distrust and cautiousness about sharing their stories as did the men. Ultimately, the context of offending revealed through the interviews provided a reality that the numbers alone are inherently unable to do.

Prior to the interviews, each individual was read a set of guidelines approved by the Human Subjects Committee at the University of Hawaiʻi at Manoa, and was asked to continue participation via a verbal consent. Verbal consent was utilized in this study so that there would be no personally-identifying record of who I had interviewed. This was the greatest level of anonymity I felt I could assure my interviewees in this situation. It was important for this population of parolees and probationers to feel absolutely secure in what they would share with me in order to achieve the highest level of validity possible. Rather than offer to send each respondent a copy of the final product, or to share results before final publication, I instructed respondents to contact me in the future for results if they were interested. While not wanting to put the onus on the subjects, I felt that this was necessary to ensure their anonymity. I did not want to keep track of any identifying information, and I explained this to them. This, in turn, seemed to add another layer of protection for the subjects.

Technically, each interview was recorded via a digital recording device and, additionally, notes were taken throughout each interview. Consistent with guidelines on human subject protection and in doing qualitative research, each interviewee was afforded the ability to refuse recording or to turn off the recorder at any point during the interview. Each interviewee was also instructed, and assured consistently throughout the interview, that they could terminate the interview at any time without penalty, and each was assured that the gift card was theirs regardless of whether or not they completed the interview, skipped questions, or decided not to go through with the interview. Each interview was conducted with flexibility in mind (Miller, 2005), which allowed for the interviewees to expand on any question or contribute new material, while still ensuring that similar material was gained from each participant.

All of the interviewees allowed me to digitally record the interviews. While I did take some notes during the interviews, I largely relied on the recorded interview audio for data capture. Upon completion of each interview, detailed notes were documented in addition to the audio recording of what each interviewee had to say. While the interviews took an average of 2 hours to complete, the entire process of compiling and analyze the data took considerably longer. The write-up of each interview, which I attempted to do immediately following each interview, took about 3-4 hours more to complete. The digital audio files were also downloaded and catalogued under the pseudonyms given each interviewee.

Once all interview data were captured, I utilized thematic coding in order to make sense of the information that had been shared with me. This is a common approach to the analysis of these data types (Miller, 2005; Gilfus, 2006). Specifically, text was analyzed for emergent patterns and themes within each of the LSI-R domains, as well as other areas that were deemed relevant to female offenders specifically (e.g., histories of abuse). In general, the LSI-R domain areas drove the themes. Emergent patterns were those that, from a sheer quantitative perspective, represented the majority (ies) response. Quotes that were ultimately used in Chapter 5 were selected on the detail they contained as well in addition to how well a particular quote exemplified an overall pattern. See Table 3.2 below for a basic demographic description of the interviewee sample.

Table 3.2 Qualitative Sample Description: Total, Male, and Female Sample

	Total (n=31)	Male (n=18)	Female (n=13)
	Percents		
Supervising agency			
Probation	32.3	33.3	30.8
Parole	67.7	66.7	69.2
Average Age	40.6	40.6	40.6
Ethnicity			
Caucasian	29.2	38.9	15.4
Hawaiian	16.1	22.2	7.7
Japanese	9.7	11.1	7.7
Filipino	3.2	0.0	23.1
Black	6.5	5.6	7.7
Indian	6.4	0.0	15.4
Korean	3.2	0.0	7.7
Samoan	3.2	5.6	0.0
Mixed Asian	6.5	11.1	0.0
Mixed	9.7	5.6	15.3
Education			
Less than high school	19.4	22.2	15.4
High school or GED	35.5	44.4	23.1
Some college	41.9	33.3	53.8
College graduate	3.2	0.0	7.7
Average number of children	1.7	1.4	2.0
Current Offense			
Violent	38.7	50.0	23.1
Property	25.8	27.8	23.1
Drugs	35.5	22.2	53.8

Interview Guides

The interviews for the parolees and probationers were semi-structured in nature. The questions were designed to target LSI-R factors and domains as well as those factors that are thought to affect recidivism for offenders generally (Jones, 1996) and for females specifically (Hannah-Moffat and Shaw, 2001; Bloom & Owen, 2002). Jones (1996, pg. 47) notes the following factors to be general predictors of continued criminal involvement, and thus were included in the interviews:

- Age at first adjudication
- Prior delinquent behavior
- Number of prior commitments to juvenile facilities
- Drug or chemical abuse
- Family relationships
- School problems
- Peer relationships

The following variables are other potential predictors of crime for both juveniles and adults, and were thus also included in the interview guides:

- Early problem behavior – e.g., troublesomeness
- Parenting and family management techniques
- Family disruption – for example, separation or divorce [note, here women more affected than men by this – economically/child-care]
- Family size and structure
- Parental or sibling criminality
- Delinquent peers
- Alcohol use
- Gender
- Personality
- Mental Health

This research not only focused on predictors of recidivism, but also in the combination of agency and structure that precipitate recidivism for offenders already caught up in the criminal justice system. Thus, these factors were also included in the interview guides. Participants in this portion of the study were not asked questions line-by-line from the interview guide. Rather, I would start with general demographic questions such as age, ethnicity, and religion. However, with the remaining areas I would ask a general question and let the individual speak freely, in an open-ended format. I obtained a wealth of information that I might otherwise have missed by not utilizing this method. I was typically able to fill in the areas outlined in the guide without having to specifically ask questions in a structured way. If I still had questions or needed clarification I simply asked those specific questions.

Conclusion

This research by no means claims to be perfect, no social science research is. However, it does represent a step forward in understanding how and why gender matters in risk/need assessment instruments and, too, why gender should matter in the *creation* and research of such instruments. The following chapters will detail the results of the traditional, quantitative based predictive validity study as well as the results of the interviews designed to get at content validity of the instrument under study. The interview data also provide rich detail that help make sense of the patterns found in the quantitative study.

This research adds to the existing literature on male and female offending by making an explicit focus on re-offending with men and women who are similarly situated, in both time and place, within the criminal justice system. It is important to note gender differences in risk to re-offend once the person has been sentenced and processed by the criminal justice system. Richie (pg. 231, 2001) notes that, "... [the] lack of knowledge about ...gender as an imperative variable in reentry has significantly limited intervention initiatives." And, Bloom et al. (pg. 77, 2003) point out that, "women respond to community supervision, incarceration, and treatment in ways that differ from those of their male counterparts... [and]...they are influenced by their responsibilities and concerns for their children, by their relationships with staff, and by their relationships with other offenders."

Ultimately, this study of the predictive and content validity of a particular risk/need assessment instrument demanded multiple methodologies. Although the predictive validity portion of this study is quite straightforward, it is an important part of assessing the appropriate use of any risk/need assessment instrument for various locations on various populations. The content validity portion of this study is less straightforward, yet just as important. The data gathered from each of these collection efforts demonstrate a different cut at a similar problem. The combination of both methods is necessary for a fuller understanding of the quality and meaning of risk/need assessment instruments for both male and female offenders.

It is hoped that the results presented in the following chapters helps inform the nature of gender and risk/need assessment instruments. And while the data derived from the interviews may or may not be some of the same individuals who have been assessed with the LSI-R in Hawai'i, these data nonetheless help provide detail, context, and greater understanding to what the quantification of criminogenic risk and need really means from men as compared to women.

CHAPTER 4

'Counting' Out of Context

If you know one con, it's just like the other.
Tim - Parolee on attitudes of parole officers toward parolees

Counting Differences in Risks and Needs

It is somewhat ironic that in a book about, in part, women ignored, the opening quote for this chapter is from a male parolee. It nevertheless seemed quite fitting, since this chapter is centered on determining whether, quantitatively, female offenders are "just like" male offenders. The literature on female offending and pathways to offending is consistently clear about the differences in male and female life experiences that bring both genders into the criminal justice system. However, recent research suggests that men and women might be more similar when it comes to desistance from crime (Sommers et al., 2006). We know that there are qualitative differences in pathways to offending between male and female offenders, but are there quantitative differences in factors related to desistance (or the opposite, recidivism), as measured via risk/need assessment instruments?

This chapter details the similarities and differences between a sample of male and female offenders who were assessed with the Level of Service Inventory–Revised (LSI-R). When viewing these figures, it is important to keep in mind that this sample of offenders does not represent a true cross-section of parolees and felony probationers in Hawai'i. Recall from the previous chapter that, in Hawai'i, all offenders on community supervision are first given what is termed a proxy[15]. The proxy is a screening instrument comprised of three items:

---

[15] The proxy was created for use in Hawai'i by Justice System Assessment and Training (JSAT) consultants.

1. Age at first arrest.
2. Number of prior arrests.
3. Current age.

The resultant data are weighted, whereby higher-scoring offenders go on to receive the LSI-R assessment and lower-scoring offenders do not. The proxy was created and adopted in Hawai'i as a method to triage cases based on risk-centered priorities. Offenders who are at the highest risk for reoffending are prioritized for treatment services as well as higher levels of surveillance. The LSI-R is the mechanism for assessing risk levels as well as for determining which services are needed (e.g., drug treatment, cognitive therapy, etc.). As mentioned in Chapter 2, the LSI-R assessment requires motivational interviewing, and thus demands greater staff time to complete. As such, the decision was made in Hawai'i to screen out the lowest risk cases and only assess the higher-risk cases, as determined by the proxy. It should be noted that this policy aligns with the risk principle of effective intervention (Andrews & Bonta, 1990).

This sample, then, theoretically represents the top 55% of the community correctional population in terms of risk for recidivism. The implications of this sample for this study are mixed. On the negative side, there may be important differences beyond the proxy items (i.e., current age, age at first arrest, and number of prior arrests) between those offenders who have been 'proxied out' and those who went on to receive the LSI-R. On the other hand, there is some control over the relative risk severity of the males and females included in this portion of the study. For example, research has been consistent regarding the impact of age and arrest history on future recidivist behavior, and these men and women are similar on these attributes.

Nevertheless, the goal here is to demonstrate whether risk/need assessment instruments designed around knowledge of male offending and validated on male-only samples are, in fact, also valid for women. What follows is an analysis of some of the similarities and differences between male and female offenders in terms of factors measured by the LSI-R, as well as a test of the predictive validity of the LSI-R for this sample of offenders sentenced to felony probation or released to parole.

Making it in the Community: Recidivism Rates

Recidivism rates, regardless of operationalization, are typically lower for females than for males[16]. This study proves no different. The rate of recidivism for females is significantly lower than for males ($\chi^2 = 3.87$, $p < .05$, Table 4.1). Nonetheless, close to one-third of both males and females did recidivate after at least one year of exposure to risk in the community.

Table 4.1 Overall Recidivism Rates by Gender (Percents)

	Female	Male
Felony Arrest or Violation of Supervision*	33.2	38.7

Note: χ^2 differences significant at the .05 level.

Table 4.2 Overall Recidivism Rates by Gender and by Agency (Percents)

	Female	Male
Probation-Only Sample		
Felony Arrest or Violation of Supervision**	33.6	40.2
Parole-Only Sample		
Felony Arrest or Violation of Supervision	28.9	29.2

Note: χ^2 differences significant at the .05 level.

The analyses presented in this chapter will treat all offenders, probationers and parolees, as one sample of community-supervised offenders. However, it is important to note the differences in recidivism

---

[16] The definition of recidivism for this study includes any felony arrest or arrest due to a violation of community supervision conditions (i.e., a technical violation).

rates between the groups (Table 4.2). In general, the differences in recidivism rates are not large between probationers and parolees, although male probationers are slightly more likely to recidivate than other groups of offenders in this sample (χ^2=4.729, p<.05). Additionally, Table 4.3 demonstrates that the differences between LSI-R scores for men and women are not significant for the entire sample or for the probation- or parole-only samples; this is similar to other research (Manchak et al., 2009). To reiterate, while recidivism rates are lower for the female offenders in this sample, and for those on probation, their overall level of assessed risk/need according to the total LSI-R scores is not significantly different. Thus, the decision remains to treat probationers and parolees as one group of community-based offenders for the purpose of this study.

Table 4.3 Overall LSI-R Score by Gender

Sample	Female	Male
Total sample	21.63	21.91
Probation-only	21.67	21.96
Parole-only	21.29	21.53

Note: Differences are not significant based on t-test for difference of means.

LSI-R Domain and Factor Differences

Recall that the LSI-R contains a total of 54 questions (items) and 10 subcomponent scales, which are typically referred to as domains. Theoretically, the higher the overall LSI-R score, the greater is the risk for recidivism. The higher an offender scores on an individual domain, the more indicative this is of a problem that needs to be treated or in which intervention should take place in order to reduce the risk of recidivism. It is instructive to begin the analysis of assessment differences between male and female offenders at this point. Are there differences between males and females on any of the items? Are there differences between males and females, overall, on the 10 domains? Not surprisingly, the answer to both is yes (Table 4.4).

Male offenders in this study scored significantly higher than females on the following domains: criminal history (t=-7.686, p<.001) and leisure-recreation ($t=-2.781$, $p<.001$). These findings are not surprising and are also similar to the Manchak et al. (2009) findings. Some of the item differences within each of these domains are noteworthy. Males are significantly more likely than women to be assessed as having had prior adult convictions ($t=-4.559$, $p<.001$), having had three or more prior convictions ($t=-5.062$, $p<.001$), having ever been incarcerated upon conviction ($t=-4.298$, $p<.001$), having experienced a revocation of community supervision ($t=-4.511$, $p<.001$), and having a record of assault or violence ($t=-10.229$, $p<.001$). Additionally, males are more likely than females to report no recent participation in organized activity ($t=-2.508$, $p<.05$) and that they could make better use of their time ($t=-2.278$, $p<.05$). One speculation here is that women are still more likely to be engaged in familial activities that may actually put them at risk due to being overwhelmed with family responsibilities - yet are scored as low risk via the instrument.

Female offenders in this sample scored significantly higher on the following domains: financial ($t=5.704$, $p<.001$); family and marital ($t=3.5.98$, $p<.01$); and emotional and personal ($t=4.716$, $p<.001$). As with the males, some of the item differences are also interesting. Females are significantly more likely to report having a reliance on social assistance ($t=8.313$, $p<.001$), having a criminal spouse or family member ($t=5.939$, $p<.001$), having past ($t=5.761$, $p<.001$) and current ($t=4.524$, $p<.001$) mental health treatment, and to having been assessed with a mental disorder that moderately interferes with daily living ($t=2.087$, $p<.05$).

There are no overall scoring differences between male and female offenders in terms of the following domains: education and employment, accommodations, and companions. Females, however, were significantly more likely to have been frequently unemployed ($t=2.148$, $p<.05$) and to have never been employed for a full year ($t=3.808$, $p<.001$) than were the male offenders.

Table 4.4 LSI-R Domain and Factor Mean Comparisons by Gender

Domain & Factors	Female	Male
Criminal History (10 points possible)***	3.45	4.54
Prior adult convictions***	.61	.73
Two or more prior convictions***	.46	.61
Three or more prior convictions***	.35	.52
Three or more present offenses	.27	.32
Arrested under age 16	.40	.43
Ever incarcerated upon conviction***	.48	.60
Escape history – institution	.05	.06
Ever punished for institutional misconduct	.16	.18
Probation/parole suspended during prior community supervision***	.33	.46
Record of assault/violence***	.33	.62
Education/Employment (10 points possible)	5.00	5.02
Currently unemployed	.62	.59
Frequently unemployed	.65	.60
Never employed for a full year**	.46	.38
Ever fired	.33	.37
Less than regular grade 10	.19	.16
Less than regular grade 12	.46	.45
Suspended or expelled at least once***	.36	.47
Participation/performance	.64	.67
Peer interactions	.64	.67
Authority interactions	.64	.68
Financial (2 points possible)***	1.20	.94
Problems	.62	.59
Reliance upon social assistance***	.58	.35
Family/Marital (4 points possible)**	1.66	1.39
Dissatisfaction with marital or equivalent situation	.34	.30
Non rewarding, parental	.39	.36
Non rewarding, other	.33	.29
Criminal family/spouse***	.60	.43

Table 4.4 continued...

Domain & Factors	Female	Male
Accommodation (3 points possible)	.82	.80
Unsatisfactory	.28	.28
3 or more address changes last year	.29	.24
High crime neighborhood	.25	.28
Leisure/Recreation (2 points possible)*	1.17	1.30
No recent participation in organized activity*	.60	.67
Could make better use of time*	.57	.63
Companions (5 points possible)	2.46	2.49
A social isolate**	.02	.06
Some criminal acquaintances	.76	.77
Some criminal friends	.63	.60
Few anti-criminal acquaintances	.51	.49
Few anti-criminal friends	.54	.55
Alcohol/Drug Problems (9 points possible)	3.14	3.34
Alcohol problem, ever***	.46	.59
Drug problem, ever	.80	.79
Alcohol problem, currently**	.15	.22
Drug problem, currently	.50	.50
Law violation*	.43	.49
Marital/family	.36	.32
School/work	.22	.25
Medical	.08	.06
Other clinical indicators	.12	.10
Emotional/Personal (5 points possible) ***	1.52	1.13
Moderate interference*	.48	.42
Severe interference	.07	.05
Mental health treatment, past***	.51	.35
Mental health treatment, current***	.24	.14
Psychological assessment, indicated*	.21	.17
Attitude/Orientation (4 points possible)	.72	85
Supportive of crime	.26	.27
Unfavorable attitude toward convention	.20	.25
Poor attitude toward sentence/conviction**	.11	.17
Poor attitude toward supervision	.15	.16

Note: Differences (t-test) in mean scores significant at the following levels:
  *p < .05, ** p < .01, ***p < .001.

Correlation with Outcome

While it is expected that there would be some differences, quantitatively, between male and female offenders on overall scoring within each of the LSI-R domains, it is important to assess how well, if at all, the LSI-R total score and the domains correlate with outcome - in this case recidivism. It is important to keep in mind that r values of .30 or greater are deemed ideal values for this type of prediction research (Van Voorhis et al., 2008). None of the reported bivariate correlations reached that value, but several were close.

The correlation between the LSI-R total score and recidivism is slightly stronger for men (r=.27, p<.001) than for women (r=.26, p<.001). Others have discovered similar male/female outcome predictions (Smith et al., 2009; Manchak et al., 2009). However, the differences in correlations with outcome for the domains are interesting, and certainly theoretically meaningful. While Table 4.5 demonstrates total LSI-R and domain scores with outcome, Table 4.6 presents a ranked comparison of the 5 domains that are most strongly correlated with recidivism for men and women.

Table 4.5 Bivariate Correlations with Recidivism for LSI-R Total Score and Domains for the Entire Sample and Male and Female Only Samples

Total LSI-R Score and Domains	Entire Sample	Male Only	Female Only
Total LSI-R Score	.27***	.27***	.26***
Criminal History Score	.10***	.09***	.11*
Education & Employment	.27***	.28***	.23***
Financial	.10***	.10***	.13***
Family & Martial	.12***	.10***	.21***
Accommodation	.14***	.15***	.10**
Leisure & Recreation	.14***	.13***	.19***
Companions	.21***	.21***	.19***
Alcohol & Drug	.21***	.20***	.27***
Emotional & Personal	.07**	.07**	.08
Attitudes & Orientation	.13***	.12***	.17***

Note: * p < .05, ** p < .01, ***p < .001

Table 4.6 Comparison of Top Five Correlates of Recidivism for Men and Women

Bivariate Correlations with Recidivism			
Men	Educational & Employment (.28)	Women	Alcohol & Drug (.27)
	Companions (.21)		Education & Employment (.23)
	Alcohol & Drug (.20)		Family & Marital (.21)
	Accommodation (.15)		Companions (.19)
	Leisure & Recreation (.13)		Leisure & Recreation (.19)

The comparison of raw scores on each of the domains, and some factors within, highlight areas in which women scored (on average) higher than men. Interestingly, only one of the areas in which women scored higher than men actually demonstrated the highest correlation with recidivism. For example, although women scored higher than men on the financial, family and marital, and emotional and personal domains, only the family and marital domain was in the top five list of correlates with recidivism ($r=.21$, $p<.001$).

The strongest domain correlation with recidivism for women is the alcohol and drug domain ($r=.27$, $p<.001$), even though this is an area in which men actually scored slightly higher than women, although not significantly so. It is also worth noting that the correlation with recidivism for this domain is slightly higher than the total LSI-R score is with recidivism. This is not necessarily surprising, since the use of drugs has been linked to self-medication or forms of mental escapism for females. For example, Gilfus (Pg. 10, 2006) notes the following with regard to female offenders, "It was usually their relational commitments and their addiction to drugs which they described as creating the conditions which necessitated their continued involvement in criminal activity."

Gilfus (2006) also documents the repeated findings of a link between substance abuse and childhood sexual abuse. The LSI-R does not, however, measure histories of abuse as either a criminogenic risk or need. This is likely a mistake. My interviews with women (Chapter

5) also document a link between childhood victimization and childhood substance abuse that continues into adulthood. Further, recent work from Van Voorhis et al. (2008) demonstrates significant correlations between current and past substance abuse, victimization, and parental stress and recidivism with samples of probationers. Childhood abuse, though, is a factor traditionally left out of actuarial risk/need assessment instruments and is one that remains somewhat controversial. Specifically, there is some debate over whether abuse represents a criminogenic need, or whether other factors represent the criminogenic/treatment need (e.g., substance abuse) while the history of abuse represents a responsivity consideration.

The education and employment domain remains a strong correlate of recidivism for women ($r=.23$, $p < .001$), but it does for men as well (it demonstrates the strongest correlation for the males in this sample). There is also a rich literature detailing the role of social capital, or lack thereof, in many aspects of life – including recidivism.

The literature would certainly suggest that a risk factor for women would be family and marital problems, and this research supports that contention. This domain on the LSI-R is also a significant predictor of recidivism for the women in this sample ($r=.21$, $p<.001$). However, this domain assesses the following categories:

- Dissatisfaction with marital or equivalent situation;
- Non-rewarding, parental;
- Non-rewarding, other relatives;
- Criminal-Family/Spouse.

It fails to fully conceptualize the issues that have been theoretically and qualitatively linked to female offending, such as familial obligations. Women involved in the criminal justice system, more so than men, are likely to be parents and may be overwhelmed by the multiple responsibilities placed upon them (Mumola, 2000). Van Voorhis' (2005) work in this area also demonstrates the importance of looking at parenting, especially at being overwhelmed as a parent.

While the presence of negative or criminal peers has always been problematic and predictive of recidivism for males, less is known about this factor with regard to female offenders. However, in this sample, the companion domain is among the strongest correlates of recidivism ($r=.19$, $p<.001$) for females. Interestingly, the companion variable, for women, is correlated with other subscales in a manner not evident with the male sample. For example, for females, the companion domain is correlated strongly with the following domains: alcohol and drug (r=.45, p<.001), accommodation (r=.41, p < .001), family and marital (r=.39, p<.001), education and employment (r=.32, p<.001) and attitudes and orientations (r=.32; p<.001). The significant correlation with recidivism, and even stronger correlation with some of the other domains, may indicate that the choice of companions for many of these women is, in fact, a criminogenic one that exacerbates other areas of risk.

It is instructive to compare those same domain correlations with the companion domain for the male offenders: alcohol and drug (r=.35, p<.001), accommodation (r=.26, p<.001), education and employment (r=.28, p<.001), family and marital (r=.22, p<.001), and attitudes and orientation (r=.21, p <.01). Although significant correlations exist here as well, they are not nearly as strongly correlated with one another as they are with the female sample.

Leisure and recreation presents the fifth-highest correlation with recidivism for females in this study (r=.19, p<.001). Lack of structured or organized time puts offenders at greater risk of recidivating. Although less predictive for males, it makes intuitive sense that a lack of structured time would correlate with negative outcomes. The interview data presented in Chapter 5 highlight that offenders view lack of structured time as a risk factor for continued offending and/or drug use because the use of drugs is a solution to boredom or loneliness that is present when time is not well structured.

In sum, alcohol and drug use, education and employment history, family and marital problems, companions, and leisure and recreation difficulties present the strongest correlations with recidivism for the female offenders in this sample. Although there is some overlap, the picture for men is different. For men, education and employment history (r=.28, p<.001), companions (r=.21, p<.001), alcohol and drug use (r=.20, p<.001), accommodations (r=.15, p<.001), and leisure and recreation (r=.13, p<.001) provided the strongest correlations with recidivism.

There is a disconnect between some domains in which the raw scores on the instrument are higher for men yet nonetheless prove to be stronger correlates of recidivism for women. This demonstrates that we do not yet fully understand the meaning of context with regard to criminogenic risk and need for females. Further, we are not fully operationalizing these risks and needs based on the wealth of existing qualitative data. This becomes imperative in places like Hawai'i and elsewhere because the actual results of the assessment, not correlations with recidivism, become the starting point for designing treatment and interventions. The highest scoring items for female offenders may not, in fact, be the areas that represent the greatest need for intervention. Further, we may not statistically understand what predictive needs mean in terms of treatment and intervention. Nonetheless, it is instructive to further explore how well the instrument performs in terms of its predictive validity by utilizing more sophisticated statistical analyses.

Survival Analyses

This section presents analyses performed using a multivariate statistical technique known as survival analysis. Survival analysis is used here in order to determine whether the LSI-R is a valid predictor of recidivism for female offenders as compared to male offenders. Survival analysis techniques are well suited for event history analyses, which describe a family of statistical procedures that measure time from a starting date (in this case, the start of community supervision) to a termination date (e.g., an episode of recidivism) within a specified period of observation. This method of analysis also controls for each offender's time at risk, which is especially important since the offenders have varying exposure times. Each offender in this study was followed for at least one year, although some offenders had up to 5 years of exposure time. Although longer follow-up periods are preferred, a one-year follow-up is acceptable since a majority (over two-thirds) of recidivism is likely to occur within the first year of exposure (Langan and Levin, 2002).

While survival analysis is the most appropriate multivariate technique for this method of data analysis, Cox regression is the actual model of survival analysis that was employed. Unlike traditional forms of multivariate regression, Cox regression allows the dependent variable to be dichotomized.

Table 4.7 Cox Regression Model 1: LSI-R Risk Levels for Total Sample and Male and Female Only Samples

	β	Exp(B)
Entire Sample		
Risk levels	.314 (.027)	1.37**
Male Only		
Risk levels	.305 (.029)	1.36**
Female Only		
Risk levels	.364 (.067)	1.44

Note: Standard errors are in parentheses. Exp(B) are the odds ratios from the model. * $p < .05$, ** $p < .01$, *** $p < .001$

Table 4.7 presents the findings of a Cox regression model, with risk levels as the only independent variable in the model. It is more instructive to analyze the odds of recidivating for each increase in risk level (the five risk levels used in Hawai'i are administrative (0), low (1), medium (2), high (3), and surveillance (4)). The odds ratios are quite small, and less intuitive to interpret, when the overall raw score is included as a predictor. For this model, each increase in risk level demonstrates a slightly better predictable outcome for females. For female offenders in this sample, the odds of recidivism increase by a factor of 1.44 ($p < .001$) for each increase in assessed risk level. For male offenders in this sample, the odds of recidivism increase by a factor of 1.36 ($p<.001$) for each increase in risk level.

Recall that at the bivariate level, each of the domains is statistically related to recidivism. However, when all domains are entered into a multivariate Cox Regression model (Table 4.8), only a few factors appear to be, net of all other, predictive of recidivism. Also recall that Cox regression simultaneously controls for the varying exposure times to risk that each offender has in the community. Again, for ease of analysis, each domain is viewed in terms of low, medium, and high score[17]. This allows for a more meaningful examination of the odds ratios for each domain in terms of the relative risk of recidivism.

Table 4.8 Cox Regression Model 2: LSI-R Domain Categories

Domain	Entire Sample β / Exp(B)	Male Only β / Exp(B)	Female Only β / Exp(B)
Criminal History Score	.06 / 1.06**	.06 / 1.07**	-.19 / 0.82
Education & Employment	.54 / 1.71***	.57 / 1.77***	.42 / 1.52**
Financial	-.14 / 0.87*	-.16 / 0.86*	.03 / 1.03
Family & Marital	-.01 / 0.99	-.04 / 0.96	.15 / 1.16
Accommodation	.05 / 1.05	.17 / 1.18	-.58 / 0.56*
Leisure & Recreation	.15 / 1.16*	.12 / 1.13	.21 / 1.23
Companions	.28 / 1.32***	.29 / 1.34***	.32 / 1.37
Alcohol & Drug	.10 / 1.12	.07 / 1.07	.28 / 1.33
Emotional & Personal	-.12 / 0.89	-.08 / 0.92	-.19 / 0.83
Attitudes & Orientation	.11 / 1.12	.12 / 1.12	.13 / 1.14

Note: Exp(B) are the odds ratios from the model.
  * p < .05, ** p < .01, *** p < .001

---

[17] With the exception of the accommodation domain. The total possible scores on this domain preclude low, medium, and high categories, so it is instead categorized as either low or high.

For the entire sample, the following domains are significantly predictive of recidivism (listed in order of the strongest predictors to the weakest: education and employment (OR=1.71, p< .001), companions (OR = 1.32, p < .001), leisure & recreation (OR = 1.16, p<.01), and financial (OR=0.87, p<.05). For the entire sample of both male and female felony probationers and parolees, scoring high on the education and employment domain proves the greatest predictor of recidivism, as does who the offender is spending time with, what they are doing with their spare time, and their overall financial status. Increases in these domains significantly increase the odds of recidivism by the amounts specified above, with the exception of the financial domain. Interestingly, higher scores on the financial domain equate to lower odds of recidivism.

When the same model is run for males only, the same basic pattern emerges; the only factor to drop out of the above analysis is leisure and recreation, which loses significance for the male-only sample. Otherwise, the same factors are significantly predictive of outcome, at roughly the same strength of prediction (Table 4.8).

The multivariate model demonstrates that, net of all ten domains in the LSI-R, only two domains are significant predictors of recidivism for female offenders in this sample. The strongest predictor is accommodations (OR=0.56, p<.05). Even though the odds ratio is less, the absolute value of the beta for this variable is larger than the other significant variable, education and employment (OR=1.52, p<.05). Interestingly for women, the higher they score on the accommodation variable, the less likely they are to recidivate. According to the LSI-R manual (Andrews and Bonta, 2000), following are the descriptions of what the highest risk offender would look like in this category:

> Accommodation is unsatisfactory: at the highest scoring level, the client is unhappy or dissatisfied with his or her accommodation situation. He or she takes no pride and makes no attempt to improve the residence. The client expresses a desire to move, and others that live there would like for him or her to move.

Three or more address changes last year: instructors are to record the number of address changes within the last twelve months, or in the year prior to incarceration.

High crime neighborhood: answer 'yes' if client resides in a high crime neighborhood, or if the neighborhood has a high proportion of offenders. Example questions may include, do the police visit your neighborhood often? Are there people in the area who are dealing drugs, doing B&Es, or fencing stolen property? Consider if the area is criminally active or opportune.

Given the categories for this domain, it is surprising that women who score *higher* on this domain are actually significantly *less* likely to recidivate. It may be that frequent moves, generally considered high risk for offenders, are actually a mechanism of escape for women in bad situations. It may also be that living in a high crime neighborhood provides an opportunity for a woman to make some underground income (e.g., prostitution, selling drugs) that goes undetected by the police, hence the correlation between high scores and lower recidivism. In other words, even though the neighborhood might not be a good one, females are still able to earn a living, even if it is untaxed and/or illegal. This is an area that future research will need to address. This also makes sense in light of the other significant factor here – the education and employment domain. Finally, it may be that even though the female offender is not happy with her living situation and makes no attempt to improve the residence, she is overwhelmed with other duties and thus neighborhood attributes do not affect her likelihood of recidivism.

Education and employment is also a significant predictor of recidivism for women, as it is for men, although the strength of the relationship is lower for females (OR=1.52, $p<.01$). It seems logical that women, as with the men, who score higher in terms of education and employment needs are more likely to be a risk for failure in the community. In terms of individual questions on this domain (refer to Table 4.4), female offenders scored highest overall on the following questions (out of 10 questions total):

1. Being frequently unemployed;

2. Participation and performance: worst is when the client hates his or job, citing reasons such as it is boring, dangerous, unpleasant, or that he or she cannot perform will. The job is a means of earning a living only, and it is not even satisfactory on those terms. The client has unreliable attendance and is often late. He or she wants to change jobs and may quit even if another job is not available;

3. Peer interactions: worst is when the client has continuous problems with coworkers and gets into fights and arguments. The client tends to remain isolated;

4. Authority interactions: worst is when the client has ongoing and significant problems and conflicts with his or her boss. The client will not follow orders and argues with the boss. The client thinks others are treated better by the boss;

5. Being currently unemployed.

Given the scores by women on this domain, and the prediction of recidivism, it appears that women have dual problems with employment – they either generally do not have employment, or legal employment, and when they do, it is unsatisfactory on several fronts. Although not significant at the .05 level, two other variables are close to demonstrating predictive validity for the female offenders in this sample, namely alcohol and drugs (OR=1.33, $p<.10$) and companions (OR=1.37, $p<.10$).

LSI-R and Ethnicity, Agency, and Type of Crime

It is also instructive to look at ethnicity in terms of predictors of recidivism, especially given the knowledge of certain ethnic overrepresentation in Hawai`i's criminal justice system. It must be noted, however, that when attempting to validate an existing instrument, ethnicity would not be considered as a predictor of risk, even if certain ethnicities demonstrate a greater likelihood of recidivism. In other words, neither ethnicity, nor gender, officially counts when assessing the risk to reoffend. The intersection of gender and ethnicity remains of sociological interest and does have implications for trajectories in the criminal justice system. With that said, adding ethnicity to the model (Table 4.9) does little to change the prediction of recidivism for the entire sample or for the male-only sample.

For the female sample, the inclusion of ethnicity does present interesting changes. Adding ethnicity to the model demonstrates that the strongest predictor of recidivism, net all other factors, is being Hawaiian/part-Hawaiian (OR=0.46, $p<.05$) and "other" (women mainly of Asian descent, OR=0.47, $p<.05$). Those female offenders are less likely to recidivate. This is a surprising finding for the Hawaiian/part-Hawaiian females given the trend for this population to be over-represented in the criminal justice system in Hawai'i. Otherwise, the accommodation (OR=0.52, $p<.05$) and education and employment (OR=1.59, $p<.01$) domains remain significant predictors of recidivism for the females in this sample.

The addition of agency, either "on probation" or "on parole," does little to alter the original findings for the Cox regression model detailed earlier (Table 4.10). The inclusion of type of crime also does little to alter the original predictors of recidivism for the sample overall, or for the males and females separately. However, property crime offenses demonstrate a significant predictor of recidivism for the sample overall (OR=1.52, $p<.001$) and for the male-only sample (OR=1.56, $p<.001$). This finding is not surprising since property offenders typically demonstrate the highest recidivism rates.

Table 4.9 Cox Regression Model 3: LSI-R Domains & Ethnicity

Domains & Ethnicity	Entire Sample β Exp(B)	Male Only β Exp(B)	Female Only β Exp(B)
Criminal History Score	.07 1.07	.07 1.08	-.17 0.84
Education & Employment	.55 1.73***	.58 1.78***	.46 1.59**
Financial	-.14 0.87*	-.15 0.86*	.06 1.06
Family & Marital	-.01 0.99	-.05 0.95	.19 1.21
Accommodation	.05 1.05	.17 1.19	-.66 0.52*
Leisure & Recreation	.15 1.16*	.12 1.13	.23 1.26
Companions	.27 1.32***	.29 1.33***	.38 1.46*
Alcohol & Drug	.10 1.11	.07 1.07	.27 1.31
Emotional & Personal	-.13 0.88	-.08 0.92	-.19 0.83
Attitudes & Orientation	.11 1.11	.11 1.12	.13 1.14
Hawaiian/Part-Hawaiian	-.03 0.97	.15 1.16	-.81 0.46*
Black	-.09 0.92	.05 1.05	-10.71 .00
Filipino	.02 1.02	.14 1.14	-.68 .51
Pacific Islander	-.02 0.98	.02 1.02	.09 1.10
Other	.07 1.07	.23 1.26	-.76 0.47*

Note: Exp(B) are the odds ratios from the model. Reference category for ethnicity is Caucasian. * p < .05, ** p < .01, *** p < .001

Table 4.10 Cox Regression Model 4: LSI-R Domains & Agency

Domains & Agency	Entire Sample β Exp(B)	Male Only β Exp(B)	Female Only β Exp(B)
Criminal History Score	.046 1.05	.060 1.06	-.240 0.79
Education & Employment	.540 1.72***	.572 1.77***	.423 1.53**
Financial	-.139 0.87*	-.156 0.86*	.078 1.08
Family & Marital	-.012 0.99	-.044 0.96	.139 1.15
Accommodation	.051 1.05	.166 1.18	-.556 0.57*
Leisure & Recreation	.153 1.17*	.121 1.13	.226 1.25
Companions	.272 1.31***	.291 1.34***	.270 1.31
Alcohol & Drug	.110 1.12	.072 1.07	.333 1.40
Emotional & Personal	-.127 0.88	-.085 0.92	-.211 0.81
Attitudes & Orientation	.109 1.12	.115 1.12	.127 1.14
Agency	.122 1.13	.040 1.04	.672 1.96

Note: Exp(B) are the odds ratios from the model.
Agency – (0=probation & 1= parole).
* p < .05, ** p < .01, *** p < .001

Table 4.11 Cox Regression Model 5: LSI-R Domains and Type of Crime

Domains & Crime Type	Entire sample β Exp(B)	Male Only β Exp(B)	Female Only β Exp(B)
Criminal History Score	.06 1.06	.07 1.07	-.20 0.82
Education & Employment	.50 1.66***	.53 1.70***	.43 1.54**
Financial	-.14 0.87*	-.15 0.86*	.03 1.03
Family & Marital	.00 1.00	-.03 0.97	.14 1.15
Accommodation	.05 1.05	.16 1.17	-.62 0.54*
Leisure & Recreation	.13 1.14*	.10 1.11	.17 1.19
Companions	.26 1.30***	.28 1.32***	.32 1.38
Alcohol & Drug	.10 1.11	.07 1.07	.30 1.35
Emotional & Personal	-.12 0.88	-.07 0.93	-.21 0.81
Attitudes & Orientation	.11 1.12	.12 1.12	.15 1.17
Violent Crime	.04 1.04	.05 1.06	-.24 0.79
Property Crime	.42 1.52***	.46 1.56***	.25 1.28
Drug Crime	.27 1.31	.25 1.29	.49 1.63

Note: Exp(B) are the odds ratios from the model. Other crime is the reference category for crime type.   * p < .05, ** p < .01, *** p < .001

Kaplan-Meier Analyses of LSI-R Risk Categories and Domains, by Gender

Kaplan-Meier analysis is a form of survival analysis that analyzes factors in terms of the time to a culminating event. Additionally, Kaplan-Meier also displays predictions of what is likely to happen to other individuals in a sample who demonstrate the same qualities as those who have already had a terminal event. In this case, the terminal event is recidivism. It is useful to demonstrate how each of the LSI-R domains delineates risk over time for males and for females in this sample. This section will present Kaplan-Meier curves for each of the LSI-R domains, as well as for the risk levels as measured by the LSI-R.

Figure 4.1 Survival Curve – Time to Recidivism, All Offenders

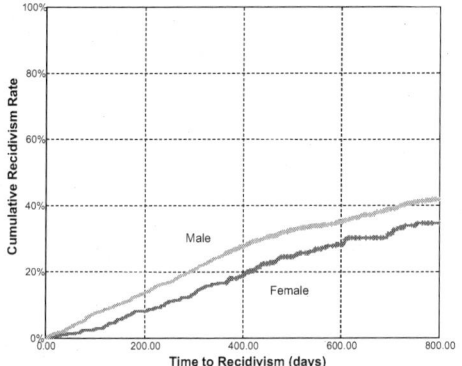

As noted earlier in this chapter, female offenders, in general, recidivate at a lower rate than do male offenders. Women also typically recidivate at a slower rate, as noted in Figure 4.1. Figure 4.2 demonstrates the time to recidivism for male and female offenders who are on probation and on parole. Recall that men on parole and probation recidivated at a slightly higher, yet insignificant, rate than did women. While there is little distinction between men and women on parole in terms of time to recidivism, female probationers do recidivate at a slower rate than do men.

Figure 4.2 Time to Recidivism, by Gender & Agency

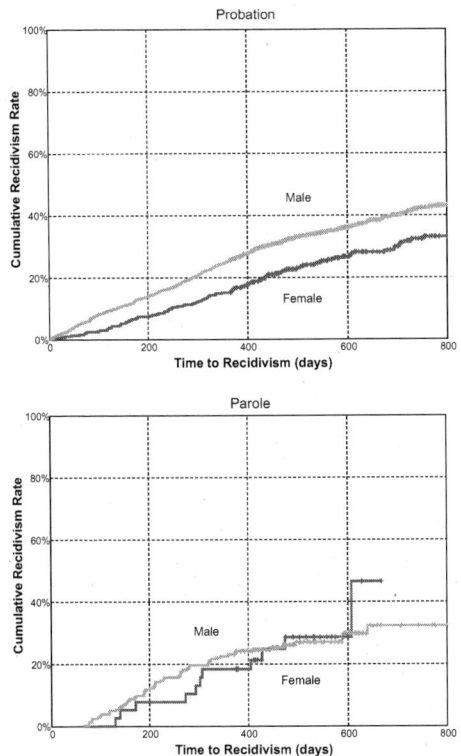

Figure 4.3 Time to Recidivism, by Classification Score & Gender

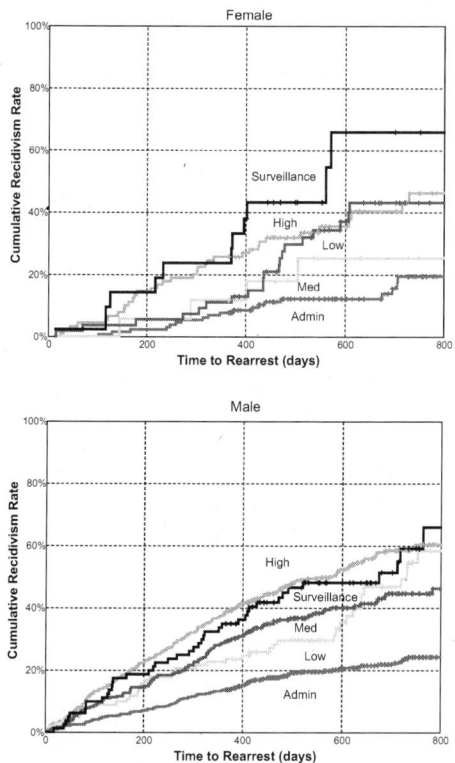

In Hawai'i, LSI-R scores are interpreted in terms of risk levels (administrative, low, medium, high, and surveillance). The Kaplan-Meier analysis demonstrates that those females who score lower, especially at the administrative level, are rearrested slower and less often than are those at higher levels (Figure 4.3). However, classification for female offenders in this sample who scored at the low and medium levels does not seem to significantly distinguish these women in terms of recidivism. The actual and predicted recidivism rates of male offenders, though, are better represented by the classification levels.

Figure 4.4 displays survival curves for low, medium, and high scores on the criminal history domain. There is little difference in recidivism patterns by domain score between male and female offenders. Offenders, regardless of gender, who scored low for criminal history clearly recidivated at both a lower and slower rate than did medium- and high- scoring offenders. However, there is little distinction between medium- and high-scoring offenders on this domain for either gender.

Figure 4.4 Time to Recidivism, by Criminal History Score & Gender

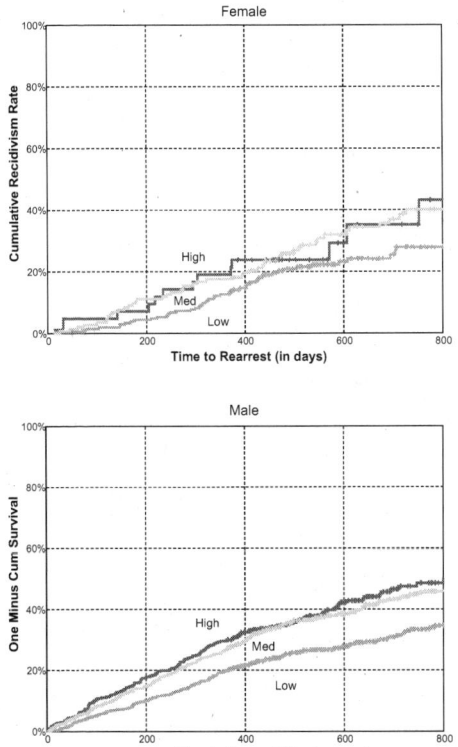

Figure 4.5 Time to Recidivism, by Education & Employment Score & Gender

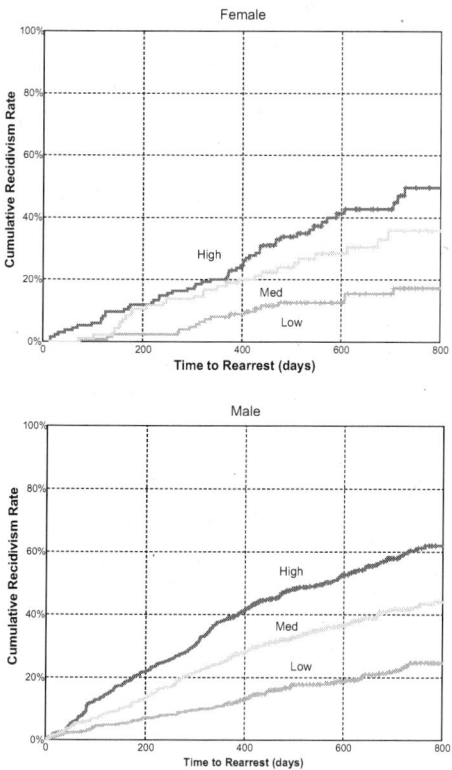

Figure 4.5 demonstrates survival curves for low, medium, and high scores on the educational and employment domain of the LSI-R. As indicated, there is a fairly clear pattern of recidivating faster and at higher rates as level of risk increases within this domain. The pattern is consistent for both male and female offenders, but delineates rate and elapsed time to the terminal event, recidivism, by score better for males than for females.

Figure 4.6 presents survival curves by low, medium, and high scores on the financial domain. Although the divergence in rates by score is statistically significant for both male and female offenders, the real distinguishing factor is between low-scoring offenders versus those who score at the medium and high levels. For both male and female offenders, there is little difference between medium- and high-scorers in terms of recidivism.

Figure 4.6 Time to Recidivism, by Financial Score & Gender

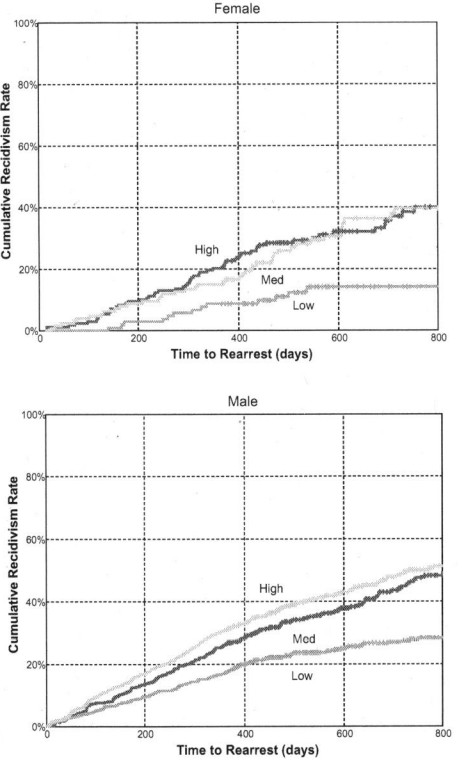

Figure 4.7 illustrates survival curves by low, medium, and high scores on the family and marital domain. For both male and female offenders, there is a distinction between low-, medium-, and high-scoring offenders in terms of recidivism. The difference in the rapidity and rate of recidivism for female offenders who score at the high level on this domain demonstrates a better divergence of scores.

Figure 4.7 Time to Recidivism, by Family & Marital Score & Gender

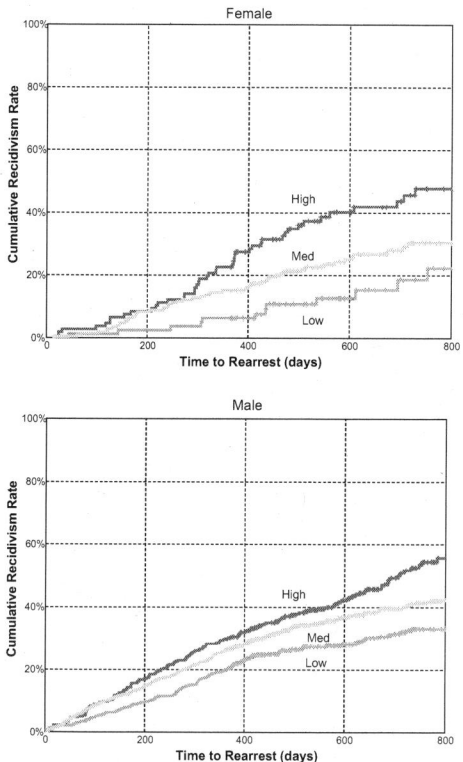

Figure 4.8 highlights differences in recidivism rates by low and high scorers on the accommodation domain[18]. These differences are statistically significant and are in the expected direction. The revocation curves demonstrate that those offenders who score high on this domain recidivate at a faster and overall higher rate than those scoring at the lower level, regardless of gender.

---

[18] There is no medium level for this domain because there were only four actual scores for all offenders, and these were collapsed into the "low" and "high" levels.

Figure 4.8 Time to Recidivism, by Accommodation Score & Gender

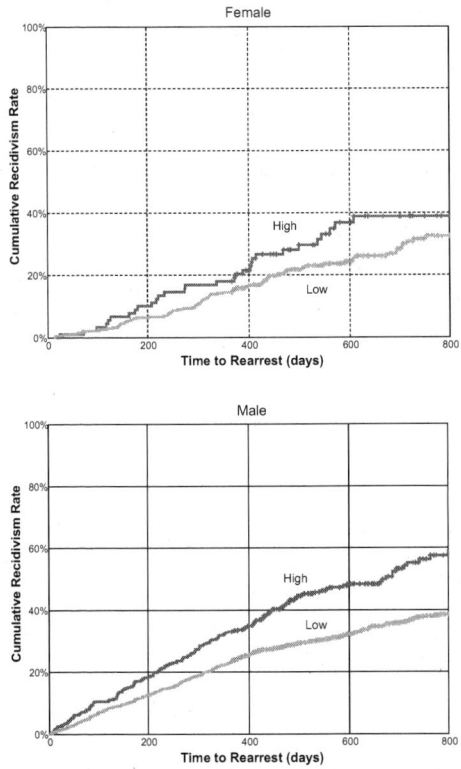

Figure 4.9 demonstrates survival curves for low, medium, and high scores on the leisure and recreation domain. Offenders, both male and female, who scored low on this factor are significantly less likely to recidivate than are those scoring at the medium and high levels. The difference in scores between high scorers and low/medium scorers is much more pronounced for female offenders in this sample.

Figure 4.10 displays survival curves for low, medium, and high scores on the companion domain. Offenders, both male and female, who scored high on this domain are more likely to recidivate than are those who score low. However, the distinction between medium and low for female offenders is not great, and the rapidity and rate of recidivism for high-scoring female offenders is more pronounced than it is for male offenders.

Figure 4.9 Time to Recidivism, by Leisure & Recreation Score & Gender

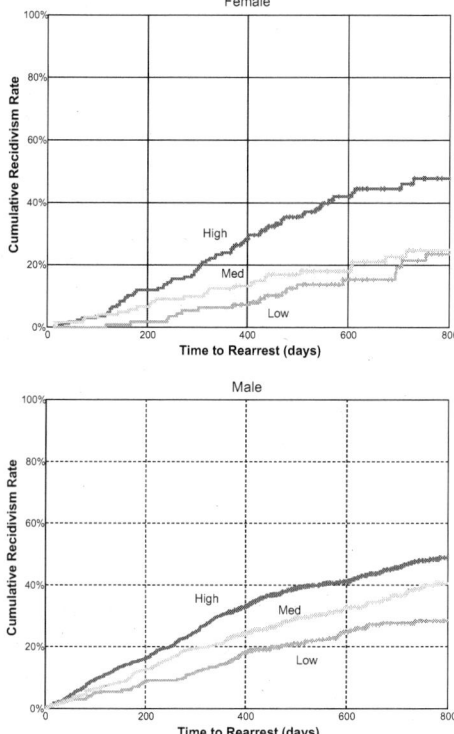

Figure 4.10 Time to Recidivism, by Companions Score & Gender

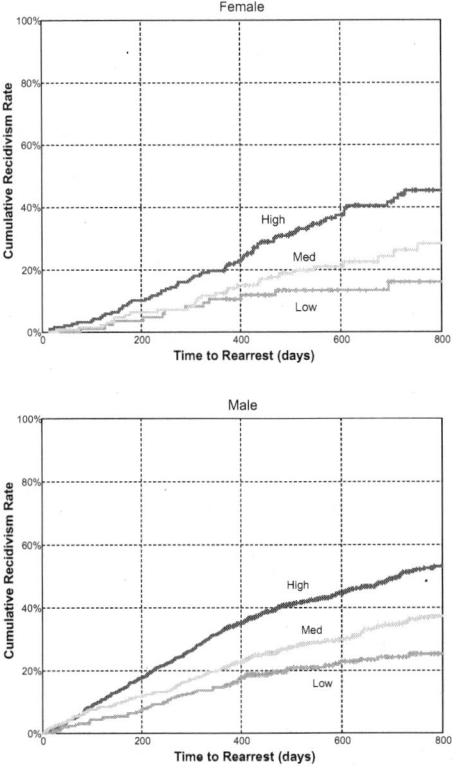

Figure 4.11 highlights survival curves for offenders who scored low, medium, and high on the alcohol and drug domain. The actual overall rates of recidivism for those who scored high on this domain are higher than for offenders scoring at the medium and low level. As with the prior two domains, the difference between the high scoring female offenders, versus low and medium scorers, is more pronounced than for male offenders in this sample. There is little difference in actual recidivism rates over time between the low and medium scoring offenders. In general, the domain does a better job at predicting recidivism by score, over time, for female offenders.

Figure 4.11 Time to Recidivism, by Alcohol & Drug Score & Gender

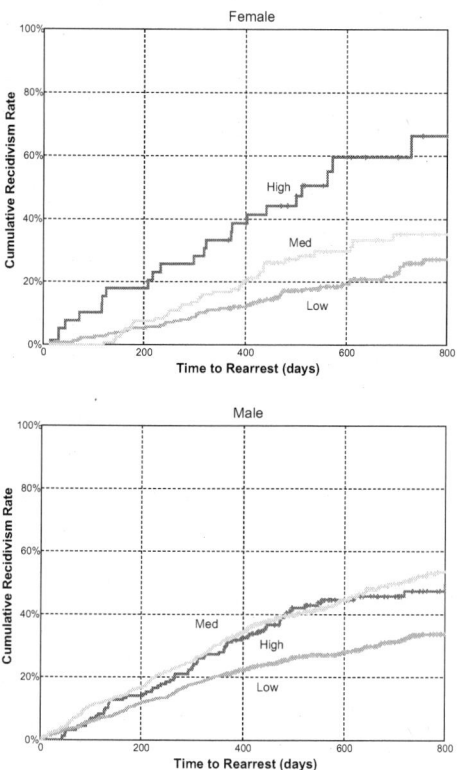

Figure 4.12 displays survival curves for offenders scoring low, medium, and high on the emotional and personal domain of the LSI-R. There is little difference in recidivism rates for these offenders, and the differences that do exist for female offenders are not statistically significant.

'Counting' Out of Context

Figure 4.12 Time to Recidivism, by Emotional & Personal Score & Gender

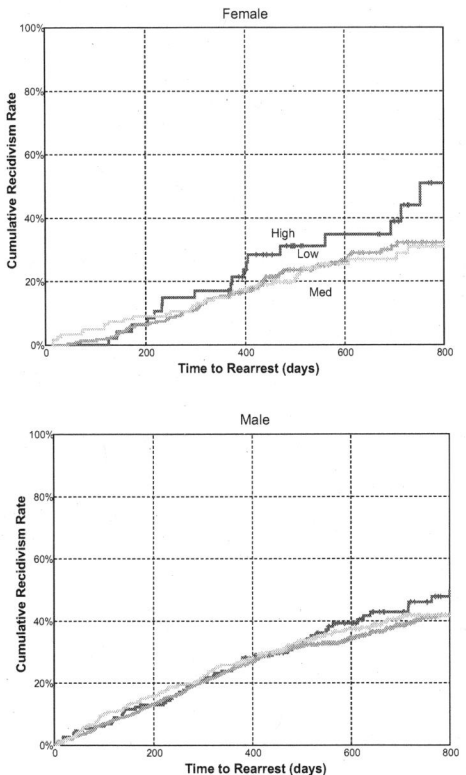

Lastly, figure 4.13 demonstrates survival curves for offenders based on their attitudes and orientation scores. Recidivism rates are in the expected direction and are significantly different, with the rates (for both male and female offenders) being highest for those who scored high on this domain and lowest for those who scored lowest. Additionally, female offenders who scored higher on this domain recidivate at an overall faster and higher rate than do male offenders.

Figure 4.13 Time to Recidivism, by Attitudes & Orientation Score & Gender

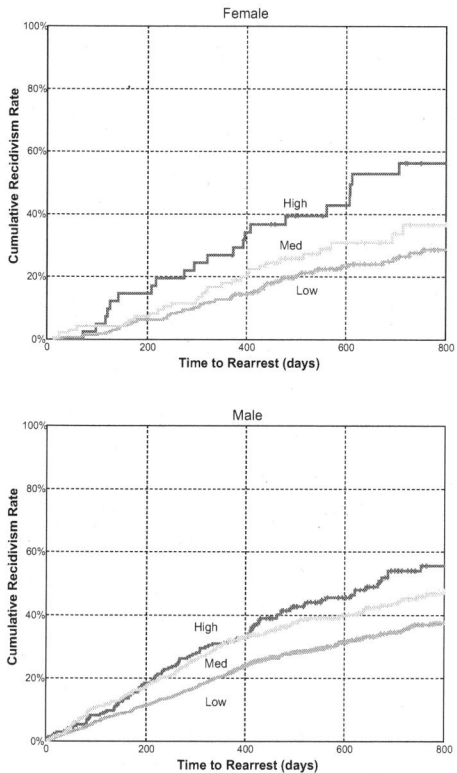

Over- and Under-Classification by Gender

One of the final factors that should be looked at when considering validation of any actuarial risk/need instrument by gender is the issue of over- and under-classification. When male and female offenders are compared based on their classification scores, the percentage of overall male and female offenders should be similar if the instrument is working the same for both genders. Figure 4.14 displays the percentage of both male and female offenders by each of the given classification levels. Although the differences are not great, there are comparatively more female offenders classified as low, high, and surveillance, and there is a slight under-representation of females in the administrative and medium categories. Overall, there is not a significant difference between male and female offenders ($\chi^2 = 4.307$, p>.05) in each of the risk levels.

Figure 4.14 Comparisons of Gender by Classification Level (Percents)

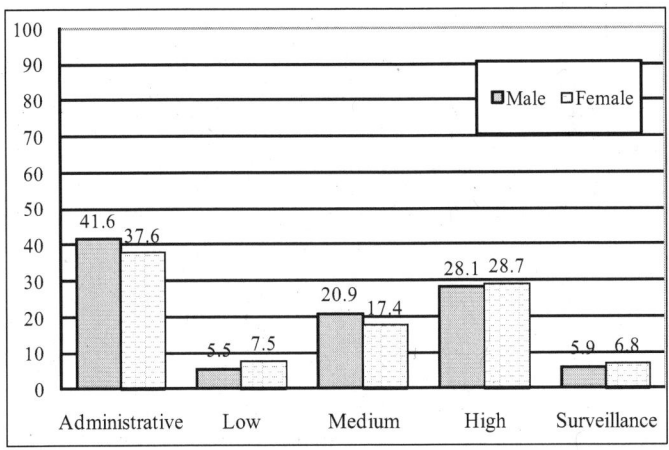

Even if the instrument is able to significantly predict recidivism, it should also demonstrate what Van Voorhis (2005) terms a 'stair step' pattern of recidivism by classification level. Figure 4.15 demonstrates the overall rates of recidivism by classification score for both male and female offenders. Although slight, some differences do emerge in terms of the percentage of offenders who recidivate at each classification level. Basically, for male offenders, the lowest recidivism rates are evident among the administrative level offenders, but the difference is not great between the low and medium or between the high and surveillance categories for the males.

For the female offenders, the recidivism rates by classification levels demonstrate that classic stair step pattern for the administrative, low, and medium levels. However, the pattern is broken by the high risk level female offenders, whereby the recidivism rates are similar (actually lower) to the rates in the medium category. For both male and female offenders, then, there appears to exist a need for an adjustment of cutoff scores by risk level.

Figure 4.15 Comparisons of Recidivism Rates by Gender and Classification Level (Percents)

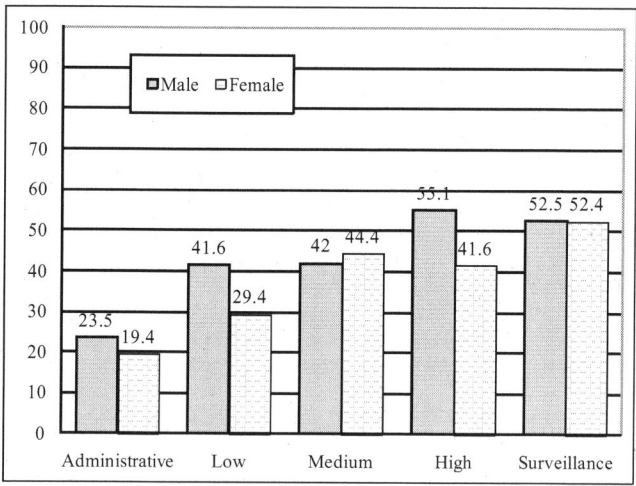

Conclusion

This chapter presented an analysis of intra/inter-gender differences with regard to the LSI-R assessments conducted on adult male and female community correctional offenders. In addition, this chapter dealt with the issue of predictive validity of this particular risk/need assessment instrument for male, and especially female, offenders. To reiterate, each offender in this sample had at least one year of exposure to risk for recidivism, and these data demonstrate that female offenders, overall, recidivated at a lower rate than did male offenders – both on probation and parole.

While the overall LSI-R scores for the females in this sample were lower than the males, they were not significantly so. This is true for the sample overall as well as for probation- or parole-only samples. However, there were some gender differences in overall scores on some of the 10 domains within the LSI-R. Namely, men scored significantly higher on the following domains: criminal history and leisure and recreation. These are the areas that are, theoretically, high risk factors for the males in this sample. Conversely, the females scored significantly higher on the following domains: financial, family and marital, and emotional and personal. Theoretically, then, these are both high areas of risk and need for intervention for the females in this sample.

However, the domains in which men and women scored highest were not necessarily the ones that were significantly correlated with recidivism. For example, even though men scored higher on the alcohol and drug domain, this proved to be a stronger correlate with recidivism for the women. In terms of predictive validity, the LSI-R was a slightly, though not significantly, better predictor of recidivism for males than for females in this sample. Similar results have been found in other studies as well (Coulson et al., 1996; Lowenkamp et al., 2001). Even though there is little difference between the predictive validity of this assessment instrument with regard to gender, it must be stressed that evaluating the predictive validity of these instruments is not the only factor to be considered with regard to gender.

How well the instrument works is equally important as *how* it works. The key factors that proved to be significant correlates, at the bivariate level, with recidivism for the females were alcohol and drug, education and employment, family and marital, companions, and leisure and recreation. The emotional and personal domain, in which women scored significantly higher than men, was the only domain not significant at the bivariate level. Especially noteworthy is the correlation between the alcohol and drug domain and recidivism for the female offenders. This domain demonstrated a slightly stronger correlation with outcome ($r=.27$) than did the total LSI-R score ($r=.26$). This may help explain why, in opposition to what the existing literature on gendered pathways would suggest, the instrument is demonstrating, roughly, the same predictive validity for women as for men. Olson et al. (2003) also found that having a substance abuse history exerted a slightly larger effect on recidivism for females as compared to males. As the next chapter will demonstrate, female offender drug use is interconnected, and often antecedent, to many of the criminogenic risk and need factors measured with the LSI-R.

The multivariate models present some interesting findings. Overall, the LSI-R proved to be a slightly, but significantly, better predictor of recidivism for the male offenders than for female offenders. While certainly contrary to my original expectations, other researchers are discovering similar results (Smith et al., 2009). Additionally, when all domains are included in a multivariate model, only two for females, as opposed to four for the males, remained significant predictors of recidivism. For the females in this sample, having unsatisfactory accommodations and moving frequently actually reduced the odds of recidivism, while a lack of social capital, measured via the educational and employment domain, increased the odds of recidivism. For men, the multivariate models demonstrated that scoring high on the education and employment, companions, and criminal history domains increased the odds of recidivism, while scoring high on the emotional and personal domain actually lowered the odds of recidivism. The addition of ethnicity and agency to the original multivariate model did not alter these patterns.

However, assessing the predictive validity of this instrument still does not definitively answer whether, in fact, there are still factors that might predict recidivism better for females. Indeed, if gender does not matter at all then we must question why there are domain differences between men and women, in this research and in others. Further, the quantification of these known correlates of recidivism for males does not necessarily signify that they *mean* the same thing for women as they do for men (Hollin & Palmer, 2006). It is imperative to assess the content validity of these items as well. This type of further exploration allows us to begin the consideration that these statistically significant correlations with outcome might be spurious in nature. If we controlled for more gender-meaningful predictors might some of these existing correlations fall out?

At face value the results here indicate that the LSI-R is meaningful for both male and females under community correctional supervision for the purpose of assigning general risk as well as assessing criminogenic need. But, the results also suggest that for treatment to be effective, we must also begin to look at causes. This, of course, is an area that demands a greater research effort. But, these data, taken in light of the existing literature and the interview data presented in the following chapter, point to the need to pay attention to causal factors that often are antecedent to the actual correlations for recidivism. Pathways to offending and desistance from offending present a complex web of both causal and correlational factors, especially with regard to gendered delinquency and crime (Belknap and Holsinger, 2006). For example, Gilfus (2006) presents data from life history analyses with incarcerated women as a means of delineating the pathway of victim to survivor to offender for many females in the criminal justice system. It seems important for us to pay attention to all three factors, especially for the female offender, yet mainstream actuarial risk/need instruments fail to account for these factors and thus may help explain some of the more specific gendered-domain and item differences.

The absence of certain gender-specific variables, such as abuse, clouds the issue of context with regard to risks for recidivism (Hollin & Palmer, 2006). For example, Belknap and Holsinger (2006, drawing from Rivera and Widom) state that "It is notable that abused and neglected girls were more likely than non-abused/neglected girls for violent delinquency offense arrests, whereas abused and neglected boys were no more likely to have violent delinquency offense arrests than non-abused/neglected boys." Further, Gilfus (2006) notes that the manner in which women respond to victimization and their relational identities both contribute to as well as aid in desistance from criminal activities. However, actuarial risk/need assessments are designed to objectively score an offender's situation on pre-set variables, thereby setting up a situation in which the context of a female offender's life might not be understood and, in many cases, not measured at all by the instrument. Not only does this complicate issues of actuarial-driven supervision, but also actuarial-driven intervention as described in Chapter 2.

Overall, these findings are certainly impacted by the exclusion of the less serious female, and male, offenders. It is likely that greater gender disparity exists but is hidden by the limitations of this sample. It may be that the women in this sample are, in a traditional sense, more like their male counterparts, since roughly half of the lower-risk women were screened out of the LSI-R assessment. Reisig et al. (2006) discovered, for example, that while predictive validity existed for women in their sample, the LSI-R was only predictive for women whose offending context paralleled that of male offenders. In that study, the LSI-R did not work well for socially and economically marginalized women who followed gendered pathways for offending. Regardless, the findings here do suggest some important gender differences in assessment in terms of outcome. The next chapter presents an analysis of what men and women have to say about the factors contained within the LSI-R, as well as factors that are considered relevant to female offending yet are not measured by the LSI-R.

CHAPTER 5

'Counting' in Context – Exploring Risk Through a Gendered Lens

Every scar on my body is drug-related.
Rose, Parolee on the role of drug addiction in her life.

The women's problems isn't the fucking addiction, it's what's behind the addiction.
Zoe, Parolee on the issues of drug abuse for women.

Introduction: Risk through a Gendered Lens

Risk is a contextual issue. In the field of actuarial risk/need assessments for correctional populations, risk is analogous to correlation. In other words, predictors of failure or success are measured by the existence of significant correlations. However, as the opening quotes for this chapter denote, especially the one from Zoe, context matters. Recall from the previous chapter that the alcohol and drug domain on the LSI-R had a higher correlation with recidivism than did the entire LSI-R score combined for the female offenders. At face value, then, the biggest need of the female offender in the community as measured via the LSI-R is alcohol and/or drug abuse treatment.

Yet, it is important to note that the contextual (and hidden) part of what is objectively measured via these risk/need assessment instruments is truly the causal side of the correlation versus causation dichotomy. For example, while drug addiction is, from a statistical standpoint, a risk factor (a correlation) for many women, and men, in this sample, the context of that addiction reveals a fairly consistent causal pathway leading to drug addiction for women - one that is not often paralleled by the men. In essence, the drug addiction/crime correlation appears to be a spurious one once other factors, especially abuse and relationships, are qualitatively factored in for females. While the LSI-R is measuring risk via correlation, the interviews suggest that correlation, and causation, in terms of what is measured, is qualitatively different for females as compared to males.

Further, the interview data reveal that some of the other LSI-R factors appear to be risk as well as protective factors, depending on the *context* in the person's life. For example relationships, especially in the lives of women, have been viewed as either risk or protective factors. The ultimate categorization depends on the context of that relationship. A similar pattern is revealed in the context of drawing financial (social) assistance and remaining unemployed while in drug treatment. Being in treatment, a protective factor, is not captured via the LSI-R. However, being on welfare, seeing a counselor or other mental health professional, and remaining unemployed are common requirements of serious drug treatment, yet are nonetheless measured as risk factors via the LSI-R. The instrument may over-classify individuals in terms of their current risk to the community by neglecting this important issue of context.

This research has identified patterns of a gendered pathway to offending, as well as how these pathways affect the content validity of a seemingly objective, quantifiable, risk/need assessment instrument. Although gender has often been left out of analyses of risk/need assessment instruments, it is an area of research that continues to develop. The data presented in this chapter indicate the need for this continued development.

While the previous chapter clearly depicts the correlates of risk (i.e., criminogenic risk/need factors) as measured by the LSI-R for men and women, this chapter begins to illustrate the other side of the correlation/causation dichotomy via a depiction of some of the salient factors in these individuals' lives that push them to offend, and to re-offend. Speaking with these male and female offenders demonstrated that early experiences as children, juveniles, and young adults, particularly for female offenders, have paved the road for existing factors, such as alcohol and drug abuse, that correlate with outcome.

The current study is quite timely as the increasing use of and dependency upon actuarial risk/need assessment instruments continues. It is important to capture not only which factors correlate with risk, but also *why* they correlate with risk. There is a plethora of information on the male offender, stemming from the traditional focus of criminology

'Counting' in Context 115

on males – from juvenile delinquents, to prisoners, to parolees. Yet, the tide has changed somewhat as more attention has been centered on the topic of women and crime. This is an important start, but it is only a start. As noted by Gilfus (2006), there is certainly more work to be done, "very few studies have been based on data obtained first hand from the women themselves in order to explore their own perceptions, experiences, and motivations for engaging in illegal activity." This study does just that, with a specific focus on how those experiences, motivations, and perceptions might potentially be impacted or neglected by risk/need instruments, instruments that seek to determine risk, or correlation, with future offending.

What follows is an analysis of what men and women said during our individual 'talk story[19]' sessions. These data are primarily organized around the ten domain areas captured in the LSI-R. The intent is to scrutinize whether criminogenic risk/need factors measured via the LSI-R demonstrate different meanings or are experienced differently for these female offenders compared to the male offenders and, if so, whether or not this affects the content validity of the instrument for female offenders.

Offender Views on Categories Related to LSI-R Domains

Criminal Histories - It's Only Illegal if You Get Caught

This portion of the LSI-R largely deals with static criminogenic risk factors. It assesses the criminal history that existed at the time of the assessment and is thus largely unchangeable. In essence, this portion of the LSI-R is concerned with past criminal behavior as it correlates with future behavior. Past experience with the criminal justice system, for many, is a strong predictor of future offending behavior. In general, the longer and more serious the criminal history, the greater the likelihood that an individual will recidivate. All of the men and women in this

---

[19] 'Talk Story' is slang in Hawai'i. It generally refers to informal conversation or storytelling and can be brief or extensive in nature.

sample were obviously caught at least once and, hence, demonstrate a criminal history and some risk of future offending. Women, in the main, exhibit less extensive and less violent criminal histories than male offenders (Hollin & Palmer, 2006; Blanchette & Brown, 2006).

What the men and women told me about their criminal histories basically parallels what official statistics demonstrate. The majority of the men committed either a crime against another person (56%) or a property crime (35%) as their instant offense. The men committed their crimes for the following reasons: to obtain money or goods (71%), personal problems (19%), or because they were high or were fulfilling some other personal gratification (2%). Most of the men committed their crimes alone (76%) and most began their criminal careers as juveniles (88%). It is not surprising that the majority of these male offenders were on parole (65%) given the high percentage of crimes against persons. The men also tended to have more arrests than did the women. Following are typical examples of men on parole and probation.

Kana is a 50 year old Hawaiian male who has spent a large portion of his adult life in the criminal justice system, including prison. He estimated that he has 11 adult arrests, but says that he would probably have had more if he had not spent so much time in prison. Kana is currently on parole for robbery and kidnapping. This is his response to my question about the factors that led to this offense:

> All these crimes happened within one period of just one month, uh, one week. It was like I gave up. Things weren't going good between my wife and I, and then she left and, and then, I just went…uh… you know, started to getting loaded and…I do a lot, you know, I do wood work and, uhm, I ended up using my knives, using my carving tools as collateral to my friend to lend me his gun and then I took the gun, and went on one crazy spree of robbing places and people….It was a give up situation…

Hector is a 24-year-old Caucasian man who estimated approximately 10 arrests as an adult. He has spent time in jail but has not been to prison. He is currently on probation for unauthorized entry into a motor vehicle and promoting a dangerous drug. Hector said the following about his crimes:

> Growing up, I had it, uh, my dad was a car salesman, he made good money, anything I wanted my dad got me. I guess it was the environment I was in, it was more, uh, the, uh, we lived in Ewa Beach. So, I mean, I met some friends and, through the time of elementary to intermediate to high school....elementary was always a (inaudible), intermediate got in and met some people who was doing some drugs an' stuff but I was never into anything. But when I got to high school, once I got to ninth grade, that's when I met the wrong crowd, I started stealing cars, started drugs.......that's what led up to it after.

While there are certainly some overlaps in what the men said with regard to their current offense as well as their criminal histories, there were also important variations between men and women.

Over half (53.8%) of the women in this sample committed a drug offense, while the remaining committed an approximately equal number of violent and property crimes. Women tended to have less serious criminal histories than did the males, and this is also reflected in the quantitative data cited in the previous chapter. The women's criminality was often situated within the context of an intimate relationship or in her substance use. In the latter case, the crime was often an attempt to obtain drugs, use drugs, or get money to buy drugs. For example, Rose is a 52 year old Caucasian woman who is on parole for drug possession and paraphernalia charges. It is important to note that Rose had a history of emotional, sexual, and physical abuse as a child. She describes the following situation as the pathway to her current offense:

> I was living in Waianae....my husband was in prison...I was with a boyfriend. I'd been with him for a few years. He knew that when my husband came out he was history. I wasn't a very nice woman, you know, it was strictly for sex and he became abusive. My husband, I've been with him 23 years, and we had drug problems but he never put his hands on me. And I really have a thing about that...you know, and I had lost my job...and, uhm, so I was on unemployment, and we were staying at Waianae in his mom's house. And his brother's came home from prison and they were very abusive and they

used to beat up their old ladies. I mean, right in the house. And it was just a matter of time that he starts slapping me. First he starts spooking me, and then he…

Rose goes on to describe that she did not know what to do and that she had alienated herself from everyone and everything but this man[20]. She ultimately left him, went to the downtown Honolulu area and began shooting dope (heroin) and engaging in prostitution to make money. Leaving this man meant that she would (and did) become homeless.

Vicki, a single Korean woman in her mid-20s, is on parole for robbery. She also had a history of abuse within her family. Her current offense was committed with others in order to obtain money for drugs. This is how she describes the factors surrounding her current offense:

…there was three people involved, including me, and we basically robbed a store, a gas station, while the people were still in there…one person had a bat, one person had a crowbar, and then I had the fake gun hidden within my jacket sleeve……my friend actually owed money to a drug dealer that she just got drugs from which I helped her smoke, and then after she was like I don't have money to pay him…and we were trying to think of ways to get money at that time….somebody brought up let's rob the gas station since they're open and I was like ok. So we used my car, picked up another person, and got all the stuff we needed, went and did it.

While the reasons, and hence the correlations with risk for recidivism, are varied for men, women tend to commit crime within the context of a dysfunctional relationship or because of an addiction to drugs, or a combination of the two. In other words, greater variation exists among the men than does among the women. And, while some of the salient factors for women may also be true for the males in this sample, certain problems appear to be endemic to the female offenders in this study. The pathway to the use of drugs is quite different for males than it is for females. In sum, while male and female offenders

---

[20] Rose is married, but her husband is currently in prison.

may commit similar acts (e.g., theft, robbery, or drug possession), the context within which they commit crimes and the motivations for them is different.

Recall from the previous chapter that criminal history scores at the bivariate level were positively correlated with recidivism for both males and females. Yet, the multivariate analyses revealed that when the other factors within the LSI-R were simultaneously considered, criminal history was no longer a significant predictor of recidivism for females, yet it remained so for males. In sum, it appears that the contextual factors of offending, closer to the causal factors, may be of greater importance for females than for males.

Education and Employment - Overworked & Underpaid

Factors related to education and employment have long been associated with recidivism (Hollin & Palmer, 2006; Blanchette & Brown, 2006), especially for offenders who are on parole (Simon, 1993). People who are well educated tend to have better jobs, and better jobs typically mean more earning potential. However, offenders, particularly those in the correctional system, do not typically represent a cross-section of the population.

The education and employment domain within the LSI-R is described as "straightforward" in terms of assessing risk for a community correctional population (Andrews & Bonta, 2000). Yet, the interviews demonstrate that this is not a straightforward section, for men or for women, but especially for the latter. The parolees and probationers in this sample are un- or under-educated and tend to have either non-existent or sporadic employment histories. Certainly, the interviews revealed an interesting assessment dilemma, at least from the perspective of scoring a risk assessment instrument. This issue will be explored further towards the end of this chapter.

Being unemployed is a risk factor, or a criminogenic need in the language of the LSI-R. However, a significant number of men and women in this sample were unemployed because they were either required or were strongly encouraged to remain unemployed while they were in substance abuse treatment and/or living in a clean and sober living environment that included a treatment component. Instead of working, they are on social assistance, which is yet another risk factor per the LSI-R. However, while being unemployed and on social assistance are criminogenic risk factors via the LSI-R, being in treatment and/or in a clean and sober house is actually a protective factor. At the time of these interviews, 44.4% of men and 61.5% of females were on welfare or other social assistance. For example, Maka is a 21-year- old part-Hawaiian male with an eleventh grade education and is currently on probation for auto theft. He is not working because he currently resides in a clean and sober house as well as attends drug treatment. Here is what he says about not working and being on social assistance:

> Right now I stay in a substance abuse program, so I gotta be on welfare. I gotta be there. I don't really like it....I don't like being with it [welfare] but, I got to, cause it's a condition I gotta follow through with. Once I complete treatment I can go work, which I like go work already, you know.

Additionally, a common requirement of both welfare and drug treatment is mental health treatment, which is also a risk factor as measured by the LSI-R. In sum, being unemployed and on social assistance is considered a criminogenic risk factor, as is any associated mental health treatment, yet these are often required of many offenders who are in an otherwise protective situation such as treatment and/or a clean and sober living situation. This is hardly a straightforward assessment of employment and may serve as a potential for over-classification.

The context of both employment and education is gendered, and again the context matters. Many of the women in this sample were abused as girls. The abuse led many of them to become truant and/or to runaway from home – a mechanism for dealing with family problems. They often gave up on their education and worked in either illegal or other historically female positions that placed them subservient to men (e.g., prostitution or the sex industry). While they may have technically been working, they were not doing so in the context of legitimate employment. Rose, for example, lost both of her parents when she was young – they both passed away from liver disease due to alcoholism. She lived in an abusive home and began to run away at an early age. She dropped out of school and began to prostitute to make money. She had her first arrest for prostitution at the age of 14. Although she did work, she had few legitimate jobs and certainly no education. It was only after being sent to prison that she obtained a GED.

Paulina, a 38-year-old mixed Caucasian/Filipina woman on parole for drug offenses, currently lives in a transitional home for families who have been or are on the verge of becoming homeless. She lives in a small studio with her husband and their 19-month-old son. She does not currently work; her husband supports them on his salary of approximately $25,000 per year. Paulina does have a work history, albeit a sporadic one. She worked in the sex industry for many years in a largely cash-only business (e.g., stripping, hostess bars, and prostitution). Here is what she had to say about her past work history:

> I was in the sex industry since I was 22, I started working in the hostess bars, and then I started stripping which, you know, uh, stripping and prostitution kind like, they offer you more money to go back with them. And even in the hostess bar situation if the rich Japanese offered me, you know, money to sleep with them I would do that. So I say sex industry 'cause it kinda covers the whole thing, and then when I started getting heavy into the heroin I just hit the streets at about, uh, God, 25, about 26, no about 25. And then the boyfriend of my first child, the one that turned me out cause, you know, he was on the run and we couldn't get like regular jobs so basically he was, like, boyfriend/pimp. Yeah, supporting his habit, so I was like the money maker, you know, so that's when I first got turned on to like, the street.

Paulina is currently not working while on parole, although she does have some educational background to speak of. She completed her high school degree and finished two years of college. She would like to return to college when her son is older. The context of her life circumstances, though, rather than a lack of work ethic appear to have guided her work trajectory.

Many in this sample lacked any education beyond a high school diploma or a GED. In fact, many of those who had obtained a GED did so largely because they were in prison. Surprisingly, the females in this sample did represent a more educated group than did the males. Only 30.8% of the females had a high school education or *less* (including

GED), compared to 72.2% of the males. The obtainment of the GED and college courses was not typical for these men or women prior to their time in prison or elsewhere in the criminal justice system. The lack of social capital in this regard was present prior to any involvement in crime or drug use, or both. This research supports past research which suggests this category to be more predictive for men than women (Blanchette & Brown, 2006). It would appear that there are some content validity issues here for the females especially, but certainly greater gender-central research is warranted.

Financial - Having an out-of-money experience

This section of the LSI-R is designed to assess the degree to which an offender has financial problems. The literature is very consistent on the extent to which an offender's financial status affects his or her propensity to offend, or re-offend. The LSI-R uses two questions to measure an offender's financial status: whether they have any financial problems (troubles meeting their basic needs, not just merely having debt) and whether they currently rely on social assistance.

Despite the fact that these measures demonstrate face validity, the interviews actually revealed an interesting contextual issue as with the employment domain - for both the men and women. While reliance on financial assistance is a risk factor, it is required for many who are currently living in a protective situation like a clean and sober environment. Additionally, being on social assistance, especially on welfare, often requires the recipient to obtain mental health treatment, which is also counted as a risk factor. However, the intent of this section of the LSI-R simply does not match the *context* of social assistance for many in this sample.

The numbers themselves are not surprising. A greater percentage of the females (76.9%) who were interviewed exhibited financial problems than did the males (61.1%). Approximately three-fifths (61.5%) of the females were currently dependent on social assistance while less than half of the men were in the same condition (44.4%).

Contrary to popular belief, only a small percentage of this sample had actually exhibited a long standing pattern of dependence on social assistance. In fact, some of the men and women I interviewed looked down on such reliance and stated that they would rather commit crimes than go on welfare in order to obtain money or goods. This seems to especially contradict the notion of social assistance as a risk factor. Not everyone fit this category, of course, as there were some who spent a considerable number of years on assistance.

Iwilani, for example, is a 43-year-old Hawaiian woman who is currently on probation for possession of drugs and paraphernalia. She neither finished high school nor earned a GED. She has been homeless for many years and has been raising a teenage boy while living out of her car. While she has been primarily responsible for her son since his birth, she has mainly done so via social assistance and drug sales. Not surprisingly, she does not have a checking account and has not saved any money. Even after receiving a substantial sum of money, Iwilani remained homeless. She co-owned some family property which her stepmother sold. Her share of the sale was $10,000. She spent this entire sum within one week. She says that she spent half on drugs and the other half on gifts for her son and other children in her family. Iwilani certainly had an inability to see how this money could have paid for a dwelling and other necessities for her and her son - for at least a short period of time. However, Iwilani has many other issues that negate her ability to earn a realistic living. She is over 40-years-old, she has no tangible assets (even the car she was living in is now gone), and although she does have a high school education she does not have any marketable skills. Further, her abusive husband left her with some disfigurement (missing front teeth[21]) that is quite noticeable and may turn prospective employers off based on her appearance alone.

The males in this sample were typically on social assistance because they were addicted to drugs prior to incarceration or sentence to probation. Some are living in clean and sober homes and are required to go to treatment and not work until they complete treatment. They are typically either on welfare or on Supplemental Security Income (SSI)[22]. For example, Jerry is a 48-year-old Japanese male who is currently on probation for theft. He finished high school and attended some college. Nonetheless, his current source of income is welfare and food stamps. He receives $418 per month from welfare and $175 in food stamps, of which $125 goes to rent (this is actually

---

[21] Iwilani's husband, who was abusive, punched her in the mouth and knocked her teeth out.

[22] Being addicted to drugs can be considered a disability and therefore allows one to draw SSI.

much cheaper than others in the sample pay in similar situations; he is part of a special Housing and Urban Development program).

Many of the females in this study were in a similar situation. Olivia is a 35-year-old French/Indian woman who is currently on probation for a drug offense. She does have a GED and a sporadic employment history. Because she has been addicted to drugs, she is currently in treatment and in a clean and sober house. She receives $418 per month from welfare, of which $360 goes to rent in the home, and all of her food stamp money also goes to the home. She says that this is not enough to live on, but "the rules of this house is that program first. Get your program done, next step is a job. You have to get a job." Yet, in the meantime, for Olivia and others like her, child support payments may be accumulating. Olivia has four children who have been cared for by others, and she will have to pay child support, including the support she missed while in jail and in treatment. Some of the women, though, had been on social assistance in the past due to issues of parenthood. At the time of these interviews, though, most of these men and women who received social assistance were doing so because they were in some type of recovery program.

In sum, the content validity of this section is questionable for both men and women offenders. Many in this study have long histories of substance abuse, and their criminal offending has been tied to addiction, especially for women. However, the LSI-R does not capture the connections between social assistance (counted as a criminogenic risk factor in the LSI-R) with treatment as it relates to either/or clean and sober housing for individuals in recovery and mental health treatment. The content of social assistance in this respect is seemingly a protective factor rather than a risk factor. Holtfreter et al. (2004) found, for example, that economically disadvantaged female offenders who did not have their immediate needs satisfied with social assistance were more, rather than less, likely to recidivate. Yet the LSI-R does not take either the context of treatment or treatment itself into account[23] and, as a result, may actually over-classify both male and female offenders in this respect.

---

[23] Save, again, mental health treatment which counts as a criminogenic risk factor.

Family and Marital Histories: A Relationship is Not Just a Relationship

The issue of family and marital factors as they correlate with recidivism has gained attention in recent years, especially given the focus on life-course theories of criminal offending (Sampson et al., 2006; Blanchette & Brown, 2006). However, while women may have traditionally been ignored in terms of general theories of offending, feminist criminologists have nonetheless been paying attention to the role of the family, marital or other personal relationships, as they relate to female offending. The LSI-R scoring manual (Andrews and Bonta, 2000, pg. 8) states that, "In general, this area is dynamic and is assessed on current marital/family interactions. There may well be historical issues from family/marital relationships that are present needs. Such needs may be noted in the Emotional/Personal area." Yet, the emotional/personal domain on the LSI-R does not specifically address the issue of past family, marital, or other intimate relationships. And, there is evidence to suggest that relationships matter not just in the present, but also in terms of pathways for involvement in crime (Belknap & Holsinger, 2006).

This research has discovered that oftentimes female offenders' relationships are criminogenic, while for men they tend to be protective. While the LSI-R does measure the satisfaction of current relationships – either marital or equivalent, it does not do much more than that. The context of the relationship for the women is left out. It is a good measure for the men as more often than not the relationship will be a dichotomous one. It is either protective or not, and does not exhibit the same complexity as with females. The data from the interviews support this. First, slightly more females (46.2%) than males (33.3%) were classified as being dissatisfied with their marital or equivalent situation. An even greater disparity existed in terms of non-rewarding relationships with parents: 92.3% for the females as compared to 72.2% for the males. Females also were more likely to have a non-rewarding relationship with other relatives (46.2% for females versus 5.6% for males). Finally, 46.2% of the females interviewed, but none of the males, had a criminal spouse or significant other.

For women, the nature of an intimate relationship is much more complicated than for men. Their histories of abuse in childhood -

which tend to travel with them into adulthood - allow some of the dysfunction and abuse of a bad relationship to become or seem normal. This clouds the issue on an LSI-R assessment if one does not probe and simply accepts at face value that what the woman has to say about the level of satisfaction with her current relationship. She may appear satisfied because she has normalized a bad relationship or abusive relationships – research has supported the tendency of abused women to minimize their victimization (Belknap, 2007). Indeed, women in this sample often defined their general well-being, both financially and emotionally, in relation to the current man in their lives.

The intent of the relationship domain in the LSI-R is to capture a criminogenic risk area that is dynamic and, thus, changeable. If one is assessed as having relationship problems, these problems can be improved and/or situations can be changed in order to reduce risk in this area. This is the objective part of a dynamic relationship via the LSI-R. Yet, for the female offenders interviewed for this study, the nature of their current relationships is very much intertwined with their past histories of childhood abuse within their own families, and abuse within their adult relationships. That some of these relationships are criminogenic is true, and the LSI-R will document if the female is currently dissatisfied with a relationship. But, what if a woman is assessed on a day in which she is feeling good about her relationship or at a time when the relationship has yet to sour? The true dynamic nature of women's current relationships is shaped by what they have learned from their abusive pasts. However, their histories demonstrate that their intimate relationships may be both protective- and risk-based, just typically not simultaneously - at least from the female's perspective. How can this be easily quantified? And, even if this were easily quantified, what is the underlying issue for these women that perpetuate these external influences (e.g., men) that are damaging to their general well-being?

It appears that the context of family and intimate others, both current (the dynamic, changeable aspect for the LSI-R) and past, are contextually different and more damaging for the females in this sample than for the males. Relationships have historically been a significant contributing factor of female delinquency and later criminality, yet these are not explicitly measured by the LSI-R. As such, the content validity of the actual risk posed by family and marital situations, for female offenders, is not realized by the LSI-R as currently constructed.

Randi is a good example of the issues and complexity surrounding relationships, especially for females. Randi is a 40-year-old Filipina woman who was convicted of robbery. The interview with Randi revealed two main factors that seem to have impacted her life. First, although she seemed to have a 'normal' family with both natural parents and five siblings, her position as the second oldest daughter in a mainly Filipino family earned her extra responsibilities. Higher expectations were placed upon her than on her siblings, especially in traditionally feminine roles such as housekeeping and helping care for the younger siblings. Second, Randi's relationships with men have not been good and seem to have greatly contributed to her offending and drug use. I asked Randi what factors were related to her criminal offending and this was her response:

Being in a bad relationship. I guess it started while I was pregnant, I was in a bad relationship, uhm, and then my husband was very abusive. So when I left him I ended up in a relationship with men, I guess I looked....I, I'm attracted to punchy, raunchy, you know, like that uhm, and it always led to me getting in trouble, always.

For Randi, both familial and intimate relationships seem to be the locus of her problems, whether direct or indirect. Her abusive relationships certainly affected her negatively. For example, she was unable to sustain employment because of physical bruises, to the face and elsewhere, that prevented her from maintaining the service type of work for which she was qualified.

What is important for this analysis, though, is the nature of Randi's relationships relative to the LSI-R. Her relationships with her parents would be scored as rewarding. Yet, the expectations placed upon her pushed her towards delinquency. At the time of this interview, Randi mentioned that she is doing well *because* of her current boyfriend. In terms of dynamic criminogenic risk, Randi would seem low risk in this situation. However, her history of being in abusive relationships is not factored into the assessment of criminogenic risks or needs. This is a mistake. For example, at the end of her interview, Randi did start to tear up as she discussed her past histories of abuse. It is clear that some of the emotional scars left from her histories of abuse are still very much with her.

Vicki is perhaps more typical of the women in this sample, in that her troubles with relationships truly began at the familial level when she was young. Vicki, a 28-year-old Korean woman on parole for robbery, was adopted when she was three years old. She spent time in foster care after that because of sexual molestation by her adoptive father. She describes a rather dysfunctional family environment that seems to continue to be problematic for her, including the denial of sexual molestation in the home, her mother's detachment, and a general feeling of not being wanted:

> [After return from foster care]: So then, I moved back in and then he started doing stuff again, and this time I called him on it. I said I know what you did last night and you should not be doing that and he just made up excuses and whatevers. So living with them was hard and then from that point I just started going downhill. Drinking, smoking, everything. Did everything.

Relationships for many female offenders seem to be iatrogenic in nature. There are both direct and indirect effects of the relationships. However, these are effects that are not easily measured and do not seem to reflect the simple questions in this section of the LSI-R. Additionally, these issues are further implicated in other areas measured by the LSI-R as being criminogenic in nature. For example, that Randi did not always maintain stable employment may not have been a function of her work ethic or ability. Rather, this was an unwanted consequence of her victimization at the hands of her intimate partner. Vicki, on the other hand, turned to drugs as a way of dealing with her relationship issues, and currently has difficulty trusting men. For women like Vicki, the LSI-R would not be able to pick up the interaction between substance use and a past history of abuse. In sum, the context of relationships for women is simply qualitatively more complex and, thus, more likely to interact with other measures – especially compared to their male counterparts.

Accommodations - A Place of My Own

Where people live can make a difference in terms of recidivism. For example, socially disorganized neighborhoods have long been associated with higher rates of crime. The accommodation portion of the LSI-R measures the level of satisfaction with current accommodations, whether or not the offender has had three or more address changes in the prior year, and whether or not they live in a high crime area. Amongst the interviewees, women were less likely (23.1%) than to men (44.4%) to indicate that they had unsatisfactory accommodations. The women and men were equally likely to live in high crime neighborhoods – 46.2% versus 44.4%, respectively. Women were more likely, however, to have had three or more address changes during the past year or in the year prior to incarceration; a little more than half (53.8%) of the women; compared to 11.1% of the men, indicated multiple address changes in the past 12 months.

The cost of living is extremely high in Hawai'i, and many people, especially the individuals represented in this sample (e.g., low education, few job skills, social assistance, poor employment histories, etc.), have a difficult time locating affordable housing. In Hawai'i it may be especially difficult to afford a rewarding living situation – at least in terms of neighborhood. A recent series of articles detail the growth of the homeless population in Hawai'i (Hoover & Perez, 2006 - *The Honolulu Advertiser)*. The first article in the series noted the growing homeless population in Hawai'i and then linked the current situation with increasing rental prices that have risen by about 90% over the past five years (Hoover & Perez, 2006). Hoover & Perez (2006) note that, "Rising prices edged a growing number of low-income renters out the door. Those lucky enough to find an available home often couldn't afford the high rent. The result was a surge of homeless people migrating toward the only place available: the beach parks." There exists in Hawai'i, then, a secondary burden of finding affordable housing, and, if that is accomplished, finding such housing in a low crime area.

There certainly seems to be a gendered pattern to frequent address changes. Indeed, frequent address changes for female offenders often reflected the relationship difficulties discussed in the previous section. Some women noted that they moved frequently in order to get away from an abusive intimate partner. It is noteworthy that many women were actually homeless prior to incarceration. They not only moved frequently, they often 'lived' in homeless situations in high crime neighborhoods. Olivia, a 34-year-old woman convicted of a drug crime, said that prior to her arrest she had been homeless. She stated that she may have occasionally stayed with a boyfriend or other, but the majority of her time was spent homeless, living on the beach. She also mentioned that this was definitely a factor that contributed to her drug use, but this becomes somewhat of a tautological statement since her drug use is also linked with her homelessness. This type of example, it seems, challenges us to further discern the true nature of these domains for women. In this instance, is it the substance abuse or housing situation that is most criminogenic? Is the homelessness a symptom of the substance abuse or a separate risk factor?

Maile, a 50-year-old local woman convicted of theft and currently living in a clean and sober house, was also homeless at the time of her arrest. This was certainly a risky situation for her. Following is what Maile had to say about her situation:

> Before I came here [current clean and sober home] I was living on Maui. I was homeless also on Maui, I was homeless for maybe....seven – eight years. Then because of the living situation, and the drugs, and, uhm, and I was doing prostitution just to get money and the drugs and stuff like that. And within those years by passing I was doing drugs I was getting into when I was doing, uhm, forging checks an stuff like that for get money and stuff.

Maile and Olivia both represent women with serious substance use problems who are simultaneously homeless. The context here suggests the latter, homelessness, to be symptomatic of substance abuse.

In sum, obtaining satisfactory accommodations (an LSI-R measure in this domain) in Hawai'i is complicated by the cost of living, especially for a population with limited earning potential. Homelessness and frequent address changes are indeed signs of trouble in terms of risk for future offending for both males and females in this sample. However, the current rental costs in Hawai'i have driven many to homelessness, as well as to frequent moves before ending up in a homeless situation. For women, this pattern is compounded by the nature of their relationships with men and their substance abuse. As such, unsatisfactory accommodations may be measuring something different for men as compared to women.

Leisure and Recreation - Occupying Time and Committing Crime

This section of the LSI-R is intended to measure how structured an offenders' time is in the community. The LSI-R scores offenders at risk for recidivism if they exhibit the absence of recent participation in an organized activity, or if they could make better use of their time. The latter measure is intended to assess whether or not an offender is bored and therefore prone to criminal behavior.

Males in this sample were more likely to report that they had an absence of participation in an organized activity than were women (72.2% versus 61.5%, respectively). There was little difference between males and females in terms of whether or not they could make better use of their time (50.0% for males and 46.2% for females). Both the males and females noted the danger of isolation, loneliness, and boredom resulting in relapse and the potential continuation of criminal activity.

Gregory, a 42-year-old Black male on parole for a burglary conviction, did not participate in any organized activities throughout his life and would have been assessed via the LSI-R as someone who needed to make better use of his time. He stated that while he does like to surf, he does not engage in that activity very much anymore. He notes that living 'in town' has hampered his ability to go surfing. Gregory grew up in Waianae but is required to stay out of that community as a condition of parole. This presents an interesting dilemma in terms of discovering risk and the context of risk. While Waianae may have been a criminogenic community for Gregory, he did engage in some pro-social activities there (namely, the surfing that was a part of his leisure and recreational activities prior to incarceration).

Randi (a 40-year-old Filipina on parole for robbery), on the other hand, does not belong to any organized club or otherwise engage in organized activities. She also would be assessed as needing to make better use of her time. She says that she does have things she likes to do, such as her nails, crossword puzzles, listening to music, spending time alone, and playing pool. However, she also notes that the absence of organized activities may contribute to her likelihood of re-offending.

Rose is engaged in organized activities and has structured her time well (mainly through attending college while she draws social assistance). She notes the problems that a lack of involvement might bring:

> Lack of community involvement was one of the big factors for me, going back downtown, or going back around the criminal element, period, that got me back into trouble because I didn't feel like I fit in anywhere.

Some of the females in this sample, although not engaged in organized activities, were quite busy in pro-social activities. Abina, for example, is a 31-year-old local girl who is on parole for robbery and a drug offense. Although she dropped out of school in the sixth grade, she has since received her GED and is currently enrolled in college[24]. She has three children. In terms of leisure and recreation, Abina said that she likes to read and to do her homework. Otherwise, she notes that she does not really have a lot of time for organized activities. Her time is actually fairly well structured right now. She is not engaged in any organized activities, but she does not view this as a risk because she is quite busy with work, school, and her children.

This section of the LSI-R does seem to have validity in terms of measuring the productive use of time. However, for offenders in Hawai'i, structured time may also be tied to particular communities, ones in which they are no longer allowed to be in as part of a condition of community supervision. Additionally, some of the offenders in this sample, especially the female offenders, may have an absence of organized activity but nonetheless exhibit structure in their time, specifically time occupied by work, school, and taking care of children. Indeed, Hollin & Palmer (2006) state this does not seem to be a criminogenic need area for women.

Companions - Hanging out with the wrong crowd

One of the best predictors of future criminal behavior, including recidivism, is whether or not one has criminal friends or peers. This is a

---

[24] Abina is much like other individuals described in the education and employment section. She only received her GED and started college after being sent to prison.

factor that has long held the attention of criminologists, as well as a statistically significant relationship with recidivism. In general, there is a positive relationship between having criminal friends or peers and the commission of crime (Blanchette & Brown, 2006). This section of the LSI-R is intended to measure the extent to which the offender's peers may contribute to his or her continued offending. There are five questions in this section assessing whether or not the offender is a social isolate, has criminal acquaintances or friends, or has an absence of anti-criminal acquaintances of friends.

Interestingly, there were very few gender differences amongst the interviewees with regard to criminal associates. Men were more likely to indicate that they were socially isolated (25%) while none of the women noted the same. In terms of criminal acquaintances, 61.1% of the males and 61.5% of the females reported having such individuals in their lives. Fewer women (46.2%) than men (55.6%) reported having criminal friends. Almost all of the men and women noted that they also had anti-criminal acquaintances or friends.

Hawai'i is a small place where people inevitably run into one another – whether desired or not. This can make it difficult to avoid social circumstances, particularly past criminal acquaintances and friends. As such, the men and women in this sample who seemed to be trying to stay out of trouble and complete community supervision with the least resistance typically devised strategies to deal with and/or avoid people who were still criminally involved, using drugs - or both. Adrian, a 29-year-old male on parole for a drug offense, notes the following:

> I still have friends and stuff that used to deal, just came out of jail, and I really don't hang with them but I still see them once in a while here and there. Uhm, I still have friends that was real close to me when I got arrested, and they still doing the same...they still using. But I try to talk to them out of it, telling them that it's not the thing that they should be doing but, you know, it's their choice.

Adrian goes on to say that his friends do not bring up the use of drugs to him. However, he probably is not pushed by his friends because he has already let them know, even if indirectly, that he is not using drugs anymore. Strategies for dealing with acquaintances and friends, rather than outright abandonment, are wise in Hawai'i, as evidenced by Adrian, "...And in Hawai'i, you cannot miss try hangin' with something. It's too small. Most of the time it's guys we grew up with each other, so it's real hard." Iwilani, a 43-year-old woman on probation for a drug offense, said that she hangs around with her sober support friends and actively avoids any of her old acquaintances and friends. She also stated that if she did hang out with them again, she knows that she would start using drugs again.

Both the men and women in this sample realized the need to stay away from negative peer pressure in order to stay crime- and drug-free. Most in the sample who were serious about getting clean or getting off of parole or probation had developed strategies to stay away from these negative influences. This section of the LSI-R appears to be applicable to both male and female offenders and does seem to exhibit content validity for both. It is worth noting, though, that Blanchette & Brown (2006) suggest greater predictive power in this area for men, and perhaps, that positive relationships are more likely to serve as a protective factor for females.

Alcohol and Drug Problems - Gone Today and Worse Tomorrow

It is not surprising that the majority of this sample exhibit addictions (or at least serious problems) with alcohol, drugs, or both. There is also a well documented connection between crime and substance abuse (Hollin & Palmer, 2006). This section of the LSI-R seems fairly straightforward and does appear to have face validity. The questions in this section center on whether the individual has now or has ever had an alcohol or a drug problem, and the extent to which either alcohol or drugs have interfered with or affected their law violations, marital/family relationships, school/work, medical health, or other negative indicators. However, the context of that connection for risk assessment has not been well documented through qualitative research. This section will detail the context of drug use in the lives of men and women serving time in the community (and what this has meant for their criminal careers). As it turns out, this seemingly straightforward section appears to be the one that is most problematic for females.

The overall use of alcohol and drugs in this sample is high. In fact, when asking about recidivism, I frequently changed the wording of my interviews to use the term relapse instead of re-offending or re-arrest, for both men and women. The connection between drug use and criminal offending was often seemingly inseparable. What follows details what this sample looks like in terms of the LSI-R measures for alcohol and drug use. While most in this sample reported that they did not currently have an alcohol problem, over half of the women (53.8%) reported having had a problem with alcohol at some point in their lives, versus 38.9% of the males. However, a full 100% of the women reported that they had a drug problem at some period in their lives versus 83.3% of the men.

The use of alcohol and drugs in this sample, as measured by the content of the LSI-R, indicate a greater impact and interference in the lives of the females than those of the male offenders. For example, *all* of the women in this sample said that drugs or alcohol had impacted their law violations, 84.6% noted that it had affected their family or marital situations; *all* noted impacts on their school or work; 53.8% noted problems with medical histories; and 69.2% had other indicators of interference (this was mainly homelessness for the females in this sample). For men, the numbers are slightly different: 83.3% noted that their alcohol or drug problems had impacted their law violations; 72.2% demonstrated that their family or marital relationships were impacted; 61.1% had their school or work affected; 22.2% had a medical problem directly related to their substance use; and 11.1% had other indicators of serious interference.

Recall from Chapter 4 that the alcohol and drug domain was a better overall predictor of recidivism for females than was the total LSI-R score. This was not true for the men. In this case, the interviews were even more important in terms of outlining *why* this is the case. The most important finding from the interviews centered on the onset of the use of drugs, namely 'guys just want to have fun and girls just want to forget.' Further, for some women, their entrée into drug use and/or their continuation was directly linked to their relationships with an intimate other.

While the context of substance abuse is not measured via the LSI-R, it was nonetheless important to uncover this context during interviews with similarly situated male and female offenders. In general, whether it was alcohol or drug use at an early age, women mainly talked about self-medication and escape while the men discussed their use in terms of partying and 'hanging out' with friends.

The circumstances of substance use and abuse for female offenders reveal an important context – use was often intertwined with issues of abuse (physical, sexual, and/or emotional) and isolation. The connection of substance use with wanting to have fun with friends stood out as a dominant pattern for the men.

Kana, a 50 year old Hawaiian on parole for a robbery and kidnapping offense, describes his history of drug use. He began using drugs at age 12. His drug experience resulted in an overdose whereby he had to have his stomach pumped. Nonetheless, he continued to use drugs by sniffing paint, smoking weed, taking acid, 'coke', and 'ice'[25]. Kana describes himself as a heavy drug user and a mainly social one. He reported no abuse as a child. Jimmy, a 31 year old part-Hawaiian on probation for robbery, said that he began using drugs at age 13. He started with pot and then moved to ice. He stated that using drugs felt good and made him feel powerful.

Olivia, on the other hand, a 35 year old on probation for a drug offense, discusses her use of drugs. She never really drank, but did begin to use drugs at the age of 15, starting with pakalolo[26], and smoking alone. She continued using, and by the age of 18 had moved to crack cocaine. After her first arrest she started using ice. Although she has not committed crime to support her habit, her use has been implicated in the removal of her four children. Her drug use seems to be directly linked to the abuse she suffered as a child and the abuse that continued into her adult life. As a child, Olivia describes growing up with a mother who was a yeller and a father who was a hitter. Her mother berated her constantly. She describes an instance as a child when she was washing dishes and her mother was waiting to hear the 'squeak' that she liked to hear. Olivia took a serrated knife and started sawing at her wrists but her mom did not really even react or take her to the hospital. She has clearly visible scars on her wrist from suicide attempts. This is what she says about the importance of drugs in her life:

> ..And, being the crack, when you smoke it goes to the part of the brain, all the rest of the brain shuts down...you don't want to concentrate, you don't want to talk, you don't want to listen just to nobody, you just want to sit there and feel that feeling

---

[25] 'Ice' refers to crystal methamphetamine.

[26] This is a term often used to describe marijuana in Hawai'i.

> because when it hits it you're, it takes over, all the rest of the brain shuts down, because it amplifies all the activity in that part of the brain. This is just my theory, now. It, it activates that part of the brain and it like, probably powers it, like amplifies it like ten times more powerful than before you took the hit....I call it a brain orgasm because it secrets more of the cerebral fluid and you just feel like your brain is floating in the middle of yourself and its, you're like, it's like... [sigh]...It takes away all your pain ....it comforts you, it makes you relax to the max.

For many women in this sample, the scars of past abuse and the other survival strategies they utilized are still quite fresh.

Rose discusses the difficulties that drugs have caused her, including stealing from friends and family to support her habit. The LSI-R would certainly pick up on this aspect of her offending. What the LSI-R does not measure, though, is the context within which Rose began to use drugs. Rose began using drugs at the age of 14. Her first drug was heroin, introduced to her by her cousin. Rose had been placed into foster care at the age of 5 and ultimately ended up with an aunt and uncle. The aunt physically abused her, quite seriously at times, while the uncle repeatedly sexually abused her. The untreated mental issues surrounding the sexual abuse are what ultimately led to her use of drugs, and then to running away, and her entrée into the world of prostitution, pimps, and other crimes designed to support her habit. Although she had thoughts of suicide, she ultimately opted to use drugs to ease her pain. This is what Rose, whose first drugs at the age of 14 were barbiturates and heroin, had to say about what drugs did for her:

> The first time I stuck it in my arm, I fell in love...I was pretty miserable, I was being molested, and my aunt was very abusive, I wanted to be with my dad. I loved my dad, regardless if how bad he was, you know. I just remember these young days driving around the country and with him while all his friends drinking, partying, and having fun, and that was the only images I had of him...happy guy...so I wanted that and, I was suffering where I was, you know, and uhm, when I shot up I didn't feel the pain that I was going

through, you know, because there was times at a young age that I wanted to commit suicide.

The different context of use between males and females becomes important since the results of the same risk/need instrument will be utilized to determine treatment needs for the offender.

While the LSI-R might do a good job in terms of identifying criminogenic risks for females in terms of their alcohol and drug abuse, the lack of context still makes this problematic. As a result, the needs part of criminogenic risks and needs (the part that makes this also a treatment oriented instrument) is rendered problematic for women. Because of the prevalent histories of abuse in the lives of women, issues of trauma, post traumatic stress disorder, and depression must be considered when shifting women into treatment. It seems that this is more than a mere responsivity issue. Rather, mental health issues seem equally important. For example, here is what Rose (who has a long history of childhood and adulthood abuse) had to say about one of her episodes of residential drug treatment:

> [after 16 months in residential treatment] I left there in a fit of rage, uhm, me and one of the male counselors…he's just very aggressive, very mean, and, uhm, I didn't know, I didn't have the, those skills to handle it, you know. So I left and I, uh, I went to [another treatment facility].

It seems feasible that any actuarial risk/need assessment instrument dealing with women would need to include histories of abuse and the impact of this abuse on substance use. This is especially important in these so-called third generation instruments that seek to include treatment as part of the assessment. The context should count.

The gendered nature of substance use for this sample cannot be understated. The men consistently discussed their use of drugs as a social event or in other masculine terms such as using it to feel powerful. Women, on the other hand, used drugs to escape problems in their lives. While the LSI-R will do a good job assessing the likelihood of risk to re-offend for these women with this domain, the same is not true with regard to defining treatment needs unless the context of trauma and abuse are factored in as well.

Emotional and Personal Problems

This section of the LSI-R measures mental health related interference in the offender's life. The manual for this section states the following (Andrews and Bonta, 2000, pg. 10): " "Interference" refers to an individual's ability to respond to life's stressors and to the quality of that person's functioning in the real word. Is his or her ability and functioning affected by psychological or psychiatric problems? Assess client's level of adaptive functioning with regard to the past year." Here, the assessment specifically measures the following: moderate interference or emotional distress (signs of anxiety or depression), severe inference or active psychosis, past or present mental health treatment, and whether a psychological assessment is indicated in the past 12 months (or whether characteristics are present, such as excessive fears, hostility, impulse control problems, etc.).

The literature on female offending has established a link between female offenders and issues of mental health, especially depression and PTSD and female offending. There is some concern over whether this section is adequate for women, especially given that the basis of this domain stems from research on mainly mentally disordered men (Hollin & Palmer, 2006). Yet, there is certainly a prevalence of mental health issues for female offenders, especially depression, anxiety, and post traumatic stress disorder. Whether these mental problems actually predict recidivism for female offenders is in question (Blanchette & Brown, 2006; Hollin & Palmer, 2006).

While only one of the males and none of the females in this sample exhibited either moderate or severe interference due to emotional and personal problems, there were other differences between males and females. All of the females reported past mental health treatment compared to roughly half of the men (55.6%). Currently, 61.5% of the women are in receipt of mental health treatment compared to only 22.2% of the males.

Given the more prevalent histories of abuse in the lives of women, it is not surprising that they are more likely to have either had mental health treatment or to currently be in treatment. As noted earlier, the scars of abuse are very real for many of these women. As such, it would seem that mental health treatment, in the past or in the present, would be a protective factor and should not count against the women in terms of risk for recidivism. Yet, the LSI-R does just that. It operates as if mental health treatment as a risk factor. However, the treatment itself does not seem to be a risk factor for the women. Rather, it is the *lack* of treatment that seems to be a criminogenic risk factor.

Zoe, a 38 year old American-Indian/Italian woman on parole for auto theft, exemplifies the need for mental health treatment, similar to many other women in this sample. She dropped out of school in the seventh grade, and her family life as well as her young and adult life are marred with extreme difficulties. Zoe lived with her mom and dad until she was 8 years old, at which time her mother committed suicide in front of her. Her dad remarried and she lived with him and her new step-mother until the age of 12, at which time she permanently ran away from home. She continued into a life of drugs, prostitution, abusive men, and crime. She has in the past and is currently engaging in mental health treatment. She says this about her mental health treatment:

> ...me, I chose to work on the most painful shit first to get, it was like well let me take a hunk out of this because this is really fucked up, first. Because it was like these were the things that I need and if I dealt with all the little, tiny little things all around the edges and then take a bite of the fucking cookie, I would never do it. So my recovery, and my trauma healing and all the things that I had went through with my therapist and still today I always deal with the largest shit first because the little shit doesn't seem that big when I start working on the big stuff. And it's not as painful, it's like working through the little scrap pieces of metal on the yards, trying to piecemeal shit together. So when you bite into the real shit, when you bite into the painful shit, when you bit into the shit that matters the most, that's when you really start your healing.

Rose also said that she has had mental health treatment, mainly for trauma but also for the diagnosis of depression and anxiety. Again, Rose had a long documented history of abuse, both as a child and as an adult, and a history of serious drug use nearly as long. Finally, Randi said that she has been in therapy in the past and is currently in therapy. She said that she is attending treatment because she is covered through her insurance and, too, because individuals at her drug treatment encouraged it as well. Randi has been in treatment for a year and states that it has been helpful.

While some men in the sample were in or had been in mental health treatment, the likelihood was less than that of women. Additionally, the context of their treatment was typically different than that of females. Kana, for example, states that he sought mental health treatment when he was on welfare, but that it was not really helpful. He had been heavily involved in drugs and crime throughout his life, but reports no abuse as a child or adult, depression, or other signs of trauma. Hector says that he never really sought mental health treatment, but did see a psychiatrist once because he needed this to qualify for his disability payments. He did not see this as helpful in any way, and has never been diagnosed with depression. Kaimi also said that he sought mental health treatment in the past, for depression and anxiety. But, he notes that he actually had to do this as part of his residential drug treatment. He does say that it was helpful, although he also notes that he did not really see any difference after treatment.

Others in this sample have certainly sought treatment in the past, but mainly because they were ordered to do so. Abina, for example, said that she sought mental health treatment when she was a juvenile because she was forced to do so as part of juvenile probation. She stated that it did not help because she did was unwilling to share anything with them at that time, other than "fuck you kind of stuff." She also stated that she has never really been diagnosed with depression, although she "set up" a fake depression diagnosis by feeding her prison psychologist signs of depression. She stated that she did not want to go to a higher level drug treatment program.

In sum, the content validity of this section for women is challenged on two fronts. First, most of the females in this sample *need* mental health treatment. The lack of mental health treatment is a real risk factor for these women. Further, the context of the mental health treatment for women is not captured via the LSI-R and thus does not exhibit content validity for these females. Secondly, for both men and women, the LSI-R does not take into account how some of the characteristics that are considered risk factors are connected. For example, many of the offenders in this sample have been or are currently in drug treatment. A common requirement is that the person remain jobless while they complete treatment - often in a clean and sober housing facility or a treatment facility. As such, even while they may be in the protective environment of a drug treatment program, they are scored as a greater risk because they are not working and are on social assistance, and may simultaneously be receiving mental health services as part of their treatment. For many of these women, the ability to seek treatment – both mental and substance – along with the financial ability to do so (albeit limited) appears quite protective and promising in the reduction of recidivism.

Attitudes and Orientation

The existence of attitudes favorable of crime, or in general a 'bad attitude,' has been a fairly standard measure in risk assessment instruments (Hollin & Palmer, 2006). The LSI-R certainly continues this tradition. This part of the LSI-R is (Andrews & Bonta, 2000, pg. 11), "...concerned with what and how a person thinks about him or herself, others, and the world. Are his or her attitudes, values, beliefs, and thinking pro-criminal and antisocial or anti-criminal and prosocial?" This section, then, scores offenders on whether they are supportive of crime, unfavorable toward convention (do they have alternatives to crime and a lifestyle favorable of crime), and whether their attitude is poor toward their sentence or toward their supervision.

While this is an area that exhibited a significant correlation with recidivism for the females in the quantitative sample and in which the females scored higher than men on average, there seemed to be little difference between the men and women who were interviewed. Only 11.1% of the men exhibited an attitude supportive of crime compared to none of the females. Few of the men and women demonstrated an attitude that was unfavorable toward convention (5.6% and 7.7%, respectively). While fewer females had negative attitudes toward their sentence (30.8% of the females versus 44.4% of the men), more had negative attitudes toward supervision 15.4% versus 11.1%).

Interestingly, most of the men and women felt good or at least "ok" about their parole or probation officers. Many also noted that the parole and probation officers had caseloads that were too high and thus were unable to devote as much time to them as they might have otherwise liked. Regardless, though, some also mentioned their distrust of sharing too much information with their parole or probation officer because of a fear of negative repercussions.

Also, almost the entire male and female sample indicated that they had normalized a conventional lifestyle to mean something similar to a stereotypical middle class lifestyle. When asked what a conventional lifestyle was, many answered having a house, a good job, a family, and the ability to take care of their responsibilities. Most also said that this type of lifestyle was very important to them. There is limited research in this area for female offenders, calling into question the predictive nature of this domain for females (Hollin & Palmer, 2006). However, data from these interviews suggest that this section appears to exhibit content validity for both women and men.

What's Left out of the LSI-R – Histories of Victimization, Health Problems, and Other

Histories of Abuse - Child Victim to Volunteer Victim

As evidenced from earlier sections, it would be neglectful, a sort of benign neglect, to discuss the issue of offending and re-offending of female offenders and not also discuss the histories of abuse, trauma, and pain in the lives of female offenders. Again, it is not to deny that male offenders, too, have these histories. But, especially in the context of actuarial risk/need assessments, the point is to look for aggregate characteristics of a group that predict recidivism and, with the newer instruments, also help define treatment needs. Disregarding the role that abuse plays in many female offenders' lives in the context of predicting risk and defining treatment needs is indeed an error in the current generation of risk/need assessment instruments, at least as applied to women.

Female offenders have greater documented histories of abuse, both physical and sexual, than do male offenders. For example, according to the latest nationally collected data on jail inmates, 55.3% of the female jail inmates have ever been physically or sexually abused compared to 13.4% of the male inmates (James, 2004). Further, abuse for women was more likely to occur both before and after the age of 18. Iwilani, one of the female probationers interviewed for this study, poignantly stated that basically, "pretty much, everyone's almost the same, it's just some get beaten up more than others."

Given the statistics cited above, it is no surprise that female inmates and probationers also exhibit higher levels of mental health problems than do similarly situated male offenders. Of the mentally ill inmates in United States prisons, 78.4% of the females had been physically and/or sexually abused compared to 32.8% of the male mentally ill inmates (Ditton, 1999).

These untreated problems often, as well, lend themselves to substance use. James (2004) reports that 34.4% of the women compared to 28.0% of the men were using drugs prior to their current jail sentence. It should be noted, though, that men were also more likely to have been using alcohol than women. The interviews from this research demonstrate a link between abuse, untreated trauma from that abuse, and to alcohol and drug use for the females that did not exist for the men – at least in aggregate terms. Past research has demonstrated a correlation between childhood abuse and delinquency (Widom, 2001) and between drug use and childhood victimization (Belknap & Holsinger, 2006, Widom & Hiller-Sturmhofel, 2001)[27]. Less attention has been devoted to looking at how those issues affect recidivism, however (Belknap & Holsinger, 2006).

In this sample of male and female offenders, many mentioned that they had received "dirty lickins" as children. I typically did not count these descriptions as physical abuse, at least when described in terms of the corporal discipline that was more often applied to children of earlier generations. In fact, most offenders in this sample did receive "dirty lickins" but also mentioned that it was in the form of punishment for something they had done - something they often felt was deserved.

The histories of abuse were nonetheless striking, especially the gendered nature of abuse. I asked about three forms of abuse in the interviews: emotional, physical, and sexual. The females interviewed here exhibited higher rates in each category. Almost three-quarters of the female offenders in this sample reported emotional abuse as a child compared to about a third of the males. A full 100% of the females reported having been emotionally abused as an adult compared to none of the men. For women, this was often in the context of an intimate relationship.

Many of the women in this sample also experienced sexual abuse as both children and as adults. Almost two-thirds, 69.2%, of the females compared to 11.1% of the males, experienced childhood sexual

---

[27] This link we be explored further in the concluding chapter.

abuse. The abuse continued into adulthood for about a third of the females (38.5%) but for none of the males. Finally, 61.5% of the females experienced childhood physical abuse compared to 22.2% of the males. Much as with the sexual abuse, the physical abuse continued into adulthood for many of the women – 61.5% of the women were abused as adults compared to none of the men. It is important to note that even with a small sample, the gender differences were statistically significant in every category. The effect of abuse in the lives of the women in this sample is worth illustrating with a few examples. Rose is a good starting point.

Recall from an earlier description that Rose is a 52 year old woman on parole for a drug offense. Rose has been involved with the justice system for most of her adult life, estimating about 100 arrests as an adult and at least 40 as a juvenile. My interview with Rose took place in her living room. At the time, she was living in a very nice and quiet neighborhood in West Oahu. The interview was in the middle of the day when many were away at work. The doors and windows were open and revealed a very quiet neighborhood on a day with a slight breeze and a light rain. I could not help notice how calm and peaceful the surrounding area was as Rose described the storm that has been her life. Her past history is so marred with abuse that it is amazing she is able to compose herself and have any period of sobriety. Yet, while she conceptualizes the physical and sexual abuse in her childhood as victimization, she says that she "volunteered" to be a victim after she ran away. She was a prostitute for many years, beginning at the age of 14, and was routinely abused by pimps and tricks, yet she does not see this as victimization. Again, she has reframed these events as a volunteerism for this lifestyle.

Rose's childhood victimization was undeniably the catalyst for both her juvenile and adult offending. It is actually quite amazing that she is making such a great recovery now. Unfortunately, the pathway from childhood victimization experienced by Rose to adult victimization is not unique, and not all are doing as well as Rose in terms of recovering from years of abuse, both personal and drug.

Iwilani, for example, is a 43 year old Hawaiian woman who is currently on probation for a drug offense. She does not exhibit the same lengthy experience with the criminal justice system as Rose, but the effect of abuse on her life is also unmistakable. Her childhood victimization, like Rose, was also the catalyst for both her juvenile and adult offending. Her dad was absent from her life and her mother constantly told her that she was not wanted. Her mom married a man who would soon after sexually assault her. As with many of the women in this sample, when she told her mother about the abuse she was accused of lying. This allowed the abuse to continue until her mom divorced her step-father. Unfortunately, she also had a cousin who sexually abused her. He advised her that if she told anyone about the abuse she would get into trouble - just as she did when she 'lied' about her step-father. She entered adulthood via an abusive relationship with her husband - the same man who ultimately introduced her to drugs.

Like most of the women I spoke to, I instantly liked Iwilani. She was motivated to complete her recovery successfully, and is quite insightful about her condition. However, there are some real concerns about her ability to be successful. Her social capital is low – she never completed high school nor received a GED, and she is over 40 now. She has been homeless for many years while raising a teenage son. Her abusive husband has left her with some disfigurement (missing front teeth) that is quite noticeable and may turn prospective employers off on appearances only. This is a fixable situation, but would take money that she simply does not have. In her case, though, her LSI-R assessment would be low risk, yet she clearly is a high risk for recidivism because of her heavy drug use and low educational and employment skills, albeit almost non-existent official criminal history.

Jackie is a 35 year old Filipina woman currently on probation for a drug offense. Jackie has four children and says that all of her kids were "ice babies." Jackie has a long history of serious drug addiction. Her drug use, though, was originally connected to her unhappy, and often abusive, family life. Jackie experienced emotional, sexual, and physical abuse as a child as well as an adult. It is worth detailing a little of what Jackie endured as a child, and later as an adult, to fully understand how a woman like this could have, for example, 4 babies born addicted to ice – and all by different fathers. Jackie experienced significant emotional abuse early on, from both her real mother and her hanai[28] mother:

> I remember in the 3rd grade, we had a contest and the contest was called build your future, and it was out of whatever you

---

[28] Hanai refers to a practice of informal adoption practices in Hawai'i.

> could possibly think of, you know, some people used the ice cream, popsicle sticks. Well for me I used legos, and, uhm, I built the future. I built a huge thing, I had to put it in a huge paper box. So, I came in 2nd place and the first three places their awards got to be displayed in the library for a month. So I remember coming home a month later with my prize, he [dad] was very proud, my hanai mom wasn't. I had placed the project onto the kitchen table. She saw that red ribbon, she, without a second of a doubt she grabbed the broom and she smashed it. And she just yelled at me and told me 2nd place was not allowed in this house.

She also experienced regular physical abuse as a child, particularly by her hanai mother:

> I got dirty lickins growing up. I got the belt, I got whatever my hanai mom could put her hands on. The minute, or the point in time I learned about running away, I went off and running.

This abuse continued for Jackie into adulthood. She entered several physically abusive relationships with men. One of these men stabbed her 8 times on Christmas Day. Here is what Jackie had to say about that relationship and the impact of the abuse:

> If you notice this scar on the right side of my face, Christmas night…..I was stabbed 8 times by my ex-boyfriend, the father of my second child. Uhm, we were well in our disease [drug addiction] uhm, but see I stayed in these relationships cause like I mentioned earlier I was stuck. was afraid of being alone. I had the low self-esteem. No confidence. No self-worth.

Jackie was largely estranged from her family due to years of emotional, physical, and sexual abuse. As such, she did not want to go to her family of origin to escape these abusive relationships. Indeed, her hanai mother did not allow her to stay at home on the rare occasions that Jackie did try to go back – even in the presence and with clear signs of physical abuse present.

Finally, Jackie discusses the issue of sexual abuse in her childhood, noting that she grew up in a family where a lot of sexual molestation occurred. She was the victim of sexual abuse at least twice as a child. She was first sexually molested at the age of 8. Here is the reaction from her hanai mother upon reporting the sexual abuse:

> I got slapped right across the face. They told me I deserved it, cause I was wearing shorts. They called me puka, which is slut. I was eight years old. So by the time that I was raped in the 7th grade, I never told anybody cause I thought it was my fault [she was raped by strangers on the way home from a school event].

It is not surprising, then, that Jackie began using drugs at the age of 13 and continued using into adulthood. Her drug use was initially connected to her family life and the issues of abuse and continued due to the lasting trauma that Jackie was forced to deal with.

This research demonstrates the difficulty that these prevalent histories of abuse, coupled with lack of treatment, pose for female offenders. And, again, the pathway for the women in this sample (and supported in other research) is one of abuse and neglect that leads to criminal offending. While the LSI-R does capture some measure of mental illness, the context of that illness, particularly trauma and depression, remains hidden behind the drug use. Following is a lengthy yet salient quote from Zoe regarding treatment, trauma, and drugs:

> They [Department of Public Safety] had a pilot program…that came up, uhm, that was relapse prevention. They had never offered services in relapse prevention in all my 20 years of experience in the Hawai'i Paroling Authority system, or the prison system. They never offered anything like that. So when that came up, I jumped on the opportunity to get in that class. And that was just before I was about to furlough, and, uhm, the other thing that they had offered was uhm, at one time, a counselor, a social worker, a family counselor that came in, and he was working at the prison in the classes, in the program area, and he offered healing and trauma, and he worked out of this book called Courage to Heal. And that book, oh my God that book, you know, but it was doing these exercises and actually digging deep, and going through the,

you know, willing to walk through the pain. And it was all on a volunteer basis. We didn't have to be there, we didn't get ordered to be there, but it was a very small group. These are 2 things that the prison had never, ever offered that I think that needed to be targeted because women, women don't, don't naturally just go out and do dope. Women go out and do dope because they're hurting.

They're trying to run from something. They're trying to run from domestic violence, or the pain, or the shame, or anger or whatever of past experiences, molestation, or whatever they've been through. They don't do drugs just because. They actually really wanna be good mothers, but something, you know, else is holding them back. So, you know, instead of targeting and saying everyone's a cookie mold level two or three, you know, what do they really need. And you know, the prison stopped the trauma classes after 15 or 16 weeks saying that it was too much of a risk [but changed the name and continued for a period].

You cannot stop somebody in the middle of healing from trauma and say, oh, I'm sorry, this has to be cancelled because it's a risk to the prison, and, uhm, the Department of Corrections wants us to stop it because something might happen. Well, they were trying to say that women were going to get overwhelmed looking at their Pandora's boxes or their issues and they were gonna become violent, or have outbursts, or hurt somebody, or kill themselves.

Zoe's insightful comments capture the truly salient issues with regard to actuarial based risk/need assessments for female offenders in the criminal justice system. Trauma, abuse, drugs, and treatment, for many women, cannot be considered separate of one another. Indeed, Blanchette & Brown (2006, pg. 109) report the following:

It is therefore suggested that female offenders' victimization histories are an important part of a holistic approach to case-based classification for effective correctional intervention. Its predominance within female offender populations in particular, often comorbid with multiple psychological/psychiatric problems and compounded by ineffectual coping, underscores the importance of offering intervention in this area.

Without the consideration of content, these male-based objective measures have the potential of yet again failing women.

Health and Children

Before leaving this chapter, other relevant issues should be discussed - ones that are important to female offenders yet are not captured in the LSI-R. The men and women in this sample were asked about any health problems they might have and any medications they might be taking. The females in this sample were about twice as likely to have current health problems as were men (61.5% and 38.9%, respectively). Not surprisingly, almost two-thirds (61.5%) of the women were taking medications compared to 27.8% of the men. These health problems, which are quite serious for some of the women (e.g., breast cancer, hepatitis C) are likely to impact their ability to address other issues, namely trauma and substance abuse. The LSI-R may over-classify these women because the instrument will score them higher due to the receipt of social assistance, mental health and substance abuse treatment, and lack of employment. The context of the women's situations will remain hidden via the LSI-R. At the very least, the added contribution of some health problems compound the demands on these women, some of which are also dealing with problems related to Child Protective Services, substance abuse treatment, and counseling.

Childcare and related responsibilities appear to affect females differently than for males. According the latest national results, roughly one half of all inmates have at least one child under the age of 18. For women, the number is higher, almost two-thirds (65.3%) have at least one child under the age of 18 compared to 54.7% of the male inmates (Mumola, 2000). Further, gender patterns are also present once the parent is incarcerated. The children of female inmates are more likely to live with relatives other than the father, whereas the father's children are overwhelmingly likely to live with the female parent (Mumola, 2000).

For this sample of offenders, 69.2% of the females had children compared to 44.4% of the men. A third of these women had their first child under the age of 18, compared to none of the men. Finally, Child and Protective Services (CPS) were more likely to have been involved in separating the mother from her children (66.7%) than was the case for the males (37.5%).

This pattern of gender disparity has implications for the female offender once she is released from prison. She is not likely to have the support of her child's father and is likely to have damaged relationships with her family. The stress of reunification with children, though, is an area not measured by these gender-neutral risk/need assessment instruments, such as the LSI-R.

Conclusion

While some of the domains in the LSI-R seem fairly straightforward and exhibit face validity, others pose problems for the offenders in this sample, especially for the female offenders. As a reminder from Chapter 4, the overall predictive validity of the LSI-R is not significantly different for the males and females in this sample. In this sense, then, men and women are technically equal in terms of the ability of the instrument to predict their future offending.

However, when the numbers are viewed with greater scrutiny, the issue of *how* each of those 10 LSI-R domains is able to predict recidivism becomes important. Especially noteworthy is the correlation of the alcohol and drug domain with recidivism, which is greater than the correlation of the overall LSI-R score with recidivism for the female offenders.

The interviews contribute to our understanding of why this might be the case. But, more importantly, what the interviews detail is the importance of *context* in assessing risk and what risk really means. As such, several domains within the LSI-R are rendered problematic for female offenders, mainly because the context of the problem is not considered. Further complicating this issue for criminogenic risk/need assessments for the female offender is that the LSI-R is not capturing all of those factors relevant to female criminality – especially in the criminogenic needs area.

This really is where the issue of correlation versus causation needs to be reviewed in the context of risk/need assessment instruments. While the LSI-R is able to determine criminogenic risk for the females, the question becomes this: what are they at risk for? Many of the women, for example, are primarily risks to themselves and their families. Like the men, they will steal or do other illegal acts to obtain money or property, often for drugs, but the correlation with recidivism seems very different than the cause[29]. It is important to make that very important distinction between cause and correlation – especially when considering treatment interventions. This distinction will be explored in more detail in the following chapter.

For now, though, it is important to note how much the context of these women's situations impacts their risk for recidivism, and their need for treatment. Context simply matters. For example, the female offenders in this sample exhibit many difficulties with relationships. If they are being assessed on a 'good' relationship day, they may score positively on this and other areas of the LSI-R. Many of these women are dependent on men (financially, emotionally, and their sense of self-worth). Although this in and of itself might be a risk factor, the context of relationships for women is not captured. What happens, for example, when this relationship goes away? While the LSI-R purports to make an objective assessment of satisfaction with current relationships (and fails to factor how this might impact a woman's financial and living situations), it is in many cases really a subjective assessment on the part of the female and is rooted in her day to day existence. The relationship is at best a positive, surviving force on the part of the female offender and at its worse it is the root of many things wrong with her life, including substance abuse and criminal offending. In a sense, women's relationships are iatrogenic in nature, and the LSI-R is not constructed to measure this in any meaningful manner.

The opening quote for this chapter came from Rose, who stated that "every scar on my body is related to drugs." For the female offender, this actually serves as a very important metaphor. The statement can be seen as a symbol of the drug as a manifestation of the scars that life has actually dealt these women. Although certainly a risk factor, the drug use for these women has mainly been used as a sort of cocoon, or protection from feelings related to histories of abuse, trauma, and depression. The drugs help in that respect, but

---

[29] Here I am only using the word cause theoretically since this study and these data are cross-sectional and cannot, therefore, empirically determine causal pathways.

simultaneously add to their histories of crime and even greater victimization.

This is actually a common theme in the literature. Take, for example, the following statement from Gilfus (2006) about one woman's pathway to crime, "Janet left home at age 14 to escape her stepfather's sexual abuse and became involved in prostitution as a teenage runaway. The resulting drug addiction and abusive domination by her male partner kept Janet immersed in a variety of street crime addiction." One could also make this a fill in the blank statement for many women in this sample: _____ left home at a young age to escape _____'s sexual abuse and became involved in drugs and crime and an abusive and controlling relationship with _____. Nevertheless, this is the type of situation that is not captured via the LSI-R yet it is nonetheless implicated in many of the domain areas for females in this sample – such as mental health, substance abuse, financial assistance, and employment. It is quite clear from this research, and others, that sexual and physical abuse marks a causal pathway into criminal offending for women in a magnitude that is not matched by male offenders. Regardless, once involved in this lifestyle, it is no longer a risk factor as captured via risk/need assessment instruments, such as the LSI-R. But it is nonetheless an area that needs to be treated or addressed (Blanchette & Brown, 2006). This is the risk that practitioners take when failing to do the requisite research and application on and to female offenders.

Zoe was quite insightful in this regard. Following is what she had to say about assessment, content, and drugs:

> The women's problems isn't the fucking addiction, it's what's behind the addiction. And if you're using one tool for screening people, in a cookie mold, and that screening is set for men [it's a problem]. Most of the women that are doing time right now are repeat offenders, most of the women are stuck in the revolving doors or recidivism. They are not targeting what they need. If you had a screening tool that targeted exactly what it was, a 9 times out of 10 you, the dead hit on the nose and the target is trauma. If you're not addressing their trauma then you can expect to be back.

While some sections of the LSI-R seem to mean the same thing for men and women, and, hence, demonstrate content validity for both, other sections have completely different meanings for men and women. The differences in content, mainly found in the educational and employment, alcohol and drugs and emotional and personal sections, may lead to over-classification. Hannah-Moffat (2009, pg. 213) cites the following:

> Collectively, the literature shows that, regardless of whether some generic "factors" (i.e., substance abuse, marital and family difficulties, and employment) are "relevant" and even "predictive for men and women, these nonspecific factors are *experienced* differently and have different effects. Tools like the LSI-R may generically categorize women's risk' however, these predictions are not firmly rooted in an empirically based understanding of female crime patterns, feminist theorization of etiology, or gendered understandings of reintegration and desistance (emphasis in original).

The differential context of female and male offending ultimately affects the content validity of this and similar instruments. The unintended consequences, though, may be hidden behind the seemingly objective scoring guide.

The first potential problem with over-classification stems from the alcohol and drug domain. To reiterate points discussed earlier, when offenders are in treatment, they are often required to remain unemployed and out of school, as well as remain on financial assistance. At face value, the LSI-R will count all of these things as criminogenic risk or need factors. Yet, if the offender is in drug treatment, it is truly a protective factor - but this is not captured or mediated by the LSI-R. While men and women may be over-classified in this regard, the case is more prevalent for women.

Further, female offenders are more likely to have had or have current mental health treatment – largely tied to their significantly more extensive histories of childhood and adult abuse. Treatment and mental health problems are considered criminogenic risk factors for offenders. Nevertheless, this should not be 'counted' *against* the female in terms of actuarial risk/need assessment. In fact, if women's pathways had been considered in the creation of the LSI-R and similar instruments, factors of abuse would be counted, as well as how these factors affect the other domain areas - such as the alcohol & drug and emotional & personal domains. The creators might consider the likelihood that mental health problems themselves surely represent a criminogenic risk, but that treatment actually negates, rather than represents, risk.

The following chapter will discuss both the predictive and content validity of the LSI-R with regard to female offenders. The case can certainly be made for the continued use of current 'gender-neutral' risk/need assessment instruments, such as the LSI-R, for females. Yet, a strong case can ultimately be made against their continued use as well. In the end, it seems that two factors come to the fore. First, if the tool is used purely for surveillance, it is likely to do more harm than good for the female. If it is used for treatment purposes it might help in some areas. Perhaps more importantly, though, are the concerns over what type of instrument we might be able to construct if we began with gender in mind – rather than gender as an assumption.

CHATPER 6

Re-Considering Female Offenders – Context Matters

The women's problems isn't the fucking addiction, it's what's behind the addiction. And if you're using one tool for screening people, in a cookie mold, and that screening is set for men [it's a problem]. – Zoe, Parolee on Risk Assessments

Introduction: Gender Matters

The opening quote from Zoe ultimately indicates the salient problems with female offenders and risk/need assessment instruments. While the quantitative analysis of offenders who received an LSI-R assessment demonstrated that the overall predictive validity for male and female offenders was similar, there were nonetheless differences in how male and female offenders scored on the individual domain areas and how these domains correlated with recidivism. This important point should not be overlooked. We would expect the domains, and correlates with recidivism, to look the same for men and women if gender simply did not matter. While predictive validity is essentially the same for males and females, the instrument does not seem to operate in a gender-neutral fashion. The alcohol and drug domain alone, for example, was more predictive of female recidivism than was the entire LSI-R score, suggesting that the instrument is indeed affected by serious content validity issues – much as Zoe's quote might suggest.

The issue of content validity becomes transparent with careful review of the qualitative data. Importantly, it is here that the significance of context emerges, the context of these 'objective' criminogenic risks and needs for males versus females. In essence, factors relevant to female offenders, especially past and present victimization, are left out. While the effects of trauma may be somewhat reflected in the alcohol and drug domain, important context is nonetheless missing. As such, women's real issues are essentially hiding in plain sight. In other words, there exists the appearance of gender-neutrality but deeper analysis reveals that this is unfortunately not the case. In terms of treatment, the use of this and similar instruments may be limited because female offenders' risk often masks the actual underlying root causes of their criminal offending – primarily centered on victimization issues.

For example, the overall use of alcohol and drugs for the men and women interviewed in this study was high. The most important finding from the interviews, though, involved the onset of drugs, namely, contrary to the song lyrics "girls just want to have fun," that guys wanted to have fun and girls just wanted to forget. In general, whether it was alcohol or drug use at an early age, women mainly talked about self-medication and escape from abusive histories or related trauma while the men discussed their use in terms of partying and in the context of peers. It is here that abuse and isolation for women became pronounced, and how their histories of abuse so aligned with their onset of substance use. Recall Rose, for example, who began using drugs at the age of 14. She stated that the first time she stuck a needle in her arm she fell in love. She had been suffering from abuse at the hands of her aunt and uncle - her primary caregivers - and the drugs took the pain away. This was a story repeated, in various fashion, by many of the women in this sample.

The men, though, often related their drug use histories, especially the onset, to a desire for fun rather than an escape from any pain or abuse. Kana, for example, a male on parole, described himself as a heavy drug user but mainly a social one. And Jimmy, who is on probation, stated that he used drugs because they made him feel good and powerful. Stated simply – male and female offenders enter and experience drug use or abuse differently.

These data indicate a fundamental problem with the LSI-R for women. Namely, although predictive validity does exist, the questionable content validity for women compared to men suggests that the tool will not be as useful for the female offender in terms of positively affecting her level of recidivism and reducing criminogenic needs via the LSI-R outcomes.

Indeed, one could make the case that the instrument tends to criminalize women's attempts to heal from quite serious histories of abuse and related trauma related. As an example, many of these domains – such as alcohol and drug and family and marital – obscured significant contextual gender differences, suggesting that the domains may indeed have content validity problems. Specifically, these domains assume a gender-neutral view of criminality that really is, in the main, a male-centered one. The general view in criminology is that drug abuse causes crime while good jobs, family, and intimate relationships lead to criminal desistance. The qualitative data here, and elsewhere, demonstrate that more females have troubled, dysfunctional (and abusive) family and intimate relationships and have more difficulties related to the feminization of poverty, including those connected to adequate accommodations. Some of these accommodation problems, too, are linked with the need to flee abusive homes and/or relationships. Drug use is the center of many of these problems, but abuse and trauma more often than not precede drug and alcohol use for female offenders.

The findings in this research also suggest that the LSI-R actually penalizes women via higher overall scores, thus higher risk classification, for behavior such as seeking help with drug abuse and trauma issues. This pattern was revealed in the qualitative data but hidden by the quantitative data. For example, many women seek mental health treatment for substance abuse and draw social assistance in the process. They are scored higher in these areas even though treatment and financial assistance seem to be protective. On the other hand, troubled intimate relationships are likely to be missed for female offenders, at least as currently measured.

The problem with relying on predictive validity alone is that you are really only able to determine whether particular pre-determined (male) factors correlate with outcome. Yet, recall that the LSI-R is intended to assess for *both* criminogenic risks and needs so as to craft viable treatment plans for offenders. If the instrument does not consider gender, the mis-identification of criminogenic needs for female offenders means that women will not get the sort of supervision and help that will *best* benefit them and public safety. In essence, the true validity for the risk/need factors currently included, and the absence of gender specific ones, may affect the overall interpretation of the instrument in ways that ultimately deny needed services to female offenders (Blanchette & Brown, 2006). There are, in short, inherent dangers in ignoring the context of female offending in ways that, at best, may fail to meet their needs or, at worst, pull them further into the system – a sort of net-widening effect. The current process of risk assessment thus serves to continue the practice of neglecting women by treating them the same as men.

The problems with content validity are, ironically, linked to the very thing that designates third generation risk/need instruments as markedly better than past ones – namely theory. The current risk/need instruments have virtually ignored the feminist research on the gendered nature of offending. While it is certainly laudable that these instruments are, in part, theoretically based, it is unfortunate that the theories of offending for a significant portion of clients, namely females, have been left out in favor of what we know about male offenders. The content validity is not at the same level as it is for men because the LSI-R was developed without attention to theoretical constructs of female offending. Rarely does one encounter criminologists, practioners, or others who question the theoretical basis upon which these instruments have been created and/or applied.

Had the designers of the LSI-R, and other similar instruments, taken gender into account, there would not be such a woeful neglect of issues that, at an aggregate level, are specific to the female offender. Any attempt to guide treatment, and hence work towards rehabilitation for recidivism reduction, might be a dubious one by treating correlates of recidivism but not getting close to the causes of such recidivism. It is difficult to tell, then, whether use of the LSI-R for female offenders might be a mirage of rehabilitation rather and a genuine effort. It can be argued that because gender specific theories were *not* considered in the creation of these instruments and, hence, the most salient criminogenic needs of female offenders are left out, that these instruments really function as second generation instruments for females. In other words, these instruments are functional for risk assessment and surveillance purposes, but not for treatment purposes. While the new penology, then, is reinforced with the assessment of female offenders, it is nonetheless challenged by assessment and treatment of male offenders with current instruments. In theory, the current assessments both assess and identify treatment (rehabilitation) needs for both genders, but in practice they only occur on a large scale for the males. The results of this study illuminate how this might be so.

The progression in risk/need assessment instruments has thus really been for men, but not for women, a pattern historically common for female offenders in the criminal justice system. This distinction is critical to the creation of gender-specific policies that will ultimately demonstrate greater validity and effectiveness for female offenders. Gilfus (2006, pg. 13) notes that "as we continue to investigate and understand the lives of women engaged in street crime, we can begin to call for criminal justice policies and programs which recognize the relationship between victimization and offending among women." This victimization is compounded by other demands uniquely, at an aggregate level, placed upon female offenders, such as child-care, economic marginality, impending homelessness, hunger, and basic needs for daily survival (Ferraro and Moe, 2006). Indeed, sufficient evidence currently exists, in this study and numerous others, to support the differential, yet equitable, treatment of the female offender. The need to consider differential treatment is often hidden behind a failure to question the epistemological basis of what we currently know about (re)offending and how this is implicated in risk/need assessments. The movement forward with so-called gender-neutral policies hides how such policies, including the use of actuarial risk/need assessment instruments, are indeed not neutral but, rather, support inequitable and inappropriate treatment of female offenders.

The interviews with the men and women in this sample indicate reason to be cautious in using the LSI-R for female offenders, at least as currently constructed. The interviews detailed the importance of *context* in assessing risk and what risk really means for female offenders as compared to male offenders. In sum, several domains within the LSI-R are rendered problematic for female offenders because the context of the problem of both risks and needs are not considered – thus the full content is not captured. These difficulties are masked, nonetheless, via the objective nature of counting and calculating risk, especially for female offenders who are considered as somehow belonging to the larger aggregate male group. Simply stated, gender should not be ignored in issues of penalty.

There exists adequate empirical and theoretical support for the existence of meaningful criminal justice related gender differences (Bloom et al., 2003). The task for criminologists, then, is to move beyond the debate over whether gender matters towards one that accounts for these known gender differences. As best stated by Maurutto & Hannah-Moffat (2007, pg. 546), "The more difficult question for law and risk assessment research is how to fairly and justly account for such contextual differences." One method of figuring this out is to continue to perform meaningful empirical work in this area, especially to determine how the context of gender matters with regard to the assessment of risks/needs and related practices (e.g., treatment and supervision) (Hannah-Moffat, 2009; Sprague, 2005; Hollin & Palmer, 2006) and how this affects content validity. Baird (2009) notes that we need to do a better job at delineating criminogenic from protective factors and failure to do so may lead to inappropriate criminal justice interventions (e.g., case planning and treatment services). This seems especially so for female offenders. Van Voorhis et al. (2008) discovered, for example, that high risk females were qualitatively different than high risk males. We simply need to consider context of female offending in risk/need instruments (Holtfreter & Cupp, 2007; Taylor & Blanchette, 2009).

In light of evidence presented here and elsewhere, it seems that the most promising approach is to move towards a decidedly gender-centered method to risk/need assessment instruments. We need to craft instruments from the ground up, beginning with a gendered lens from creation through validation and ultimate use (Van Voorhis et al., 2008; Kelly & Blanchette, 2009; Hannah-Moffat, 2009; Blanchette & Brown, 2006). If we did this we would likely end up with instruments that look different than the current gender-neutral ones (Van Voorhis et al., 2008; Holtfreter & Cupp, 2007). The emergence of so-called fourth generation instruments, which incorporate strengths and protective factors, seem more appropriate for female offenders, especially given their lower risk relative to men (Blanchette & Brown, 2006). Further, this seems a positive move away from the current gender-neutral model which criminalizes women's trauma-related survival strategies (Bloom et al. 2003).

These gender-responsive instruments would likely incorporate contextual differences, including those related to victimization, trauma, mental health (such as depression and anxiety), familial and intimate relationships, self-esteem, self-efficacy, parental and caregiver needs, and issues related to the feminization of poverty (Blanchette & Brown, 2006; Deschenes et al., 2006). Indeed, gender-related items have been empirically linked to outcome, including strength-based measures (Van Voorhis et al., 2008; Bloom et al., 2003), so this route seems unlikely to negatively impact public safety. This approach does require an accounting of the context of female offending and criminogenic risks and needs.

Cause, Correlation, and Context in Risk/Need Assessments

It appears that any discussion of actuarial risk/need assessment instruments for females must consider three 'C's with regard to recidivism prediction and treatment need identification: correlation, causation, and context. One problem with the risk/need assessment movement, historically, has been the failure to take into account theoretical causes of crime, rather than merely correlates of crime.

Instruments such as the LSI-R, though, have moved beyond that criticism via the inclusion of theory in its creation. However, like most mainstream criminology theories, the theoretical basis (social learning theory) was crafted on knowledge of male offending. Rather than question whether theories of female criminality might be different and/or important, the creators of the LSI-R assumed a one-size fits all approach to the theoretical basis of their risk/need assessment. This is problematic, though, since risk/need assessment instruments ultimately classify and manage risk based on *correlates* of recidivism. And, as already exemplified here, the correlates on most contemporary risk assessment instruments are aggregate correlates of offending for male offenders and have failed to take into account contextual differences between males and females (Reisig et al., 2006).

Just because there is a correlation between two factors does not mean that one factor causes the other - correlation is not causation (Goertzel, 2002). Although the LSI-R demonstrates significant domain correlations with recidivism for female offenders, some of these correlations may be spurious in nature, especially in the case of the alcohol and drug domain. Harcourt (2007, pg. 190) offers the following regarding actuarial methods and the dependence on correlations, "It magnifies correlations into carceral distortions."

Herein lies the problem with failing to count from a feminist perspective and the failure to consider theories of female offending in the construction of risk/need instruments. The focus on aggregate correlations with recidivism from largely male samples, with variables measured from constructs of largely male theories, ultimately distorts the picture for females. Counting attributes of the offenders represented in this sample, for example, masks important pushes to offending and drug use for men (who want to have fun) and women (who want to forget). Regardless, the results of the counts (via the LSI-R assessment) will ultimately guide the manner in which *both* are supervised and case managed. Hidden behind these counts, though, are the trauma and abuse that push many women into the system, often via substance abuse.

Although there is no perfect measurement approach for any social science research project, Sprague (2005) reminds us that "every measurement approach creates a pattern of selective visibility: it taps some aspect of a phenomenon and hides others." Further, what remains hidden is shaped by historical and political contexts within which measurements are decided (Sprague, 2005). Within the realm of both criminological theory generally and the related creation of actuarial risk/need assessment instruments specifically, this has been a largely male-centered context. What we know, in the main, about correlates of (re)offending is mainly what we know about male (re)offending. When females have been included in research it has primarily been via the inclusion of larger datasets in which male offenders dominate the numbers and, thus, dominate the statistical outcomes. In this case, gender specific attributes are selectively invisible. These results, as elsewhere, demonstrate what Zoe's comment at the beginning of this chapter might suggest – if we simply allow women's voices to emerge they do tell us their needs – and those needs are often related to childhood and adult victimization, relationships, and poverty (Holtfreter & Cupp, 2007).

Ultimately, though, issues surrounding correlation present only one part of a larger problem. What is often left out of these discussions about instrument validity are the other two Cs, namely causes and context. The assessment of risk/needs from an actuarial standpoint cannot assess cause, but the context of offending is also ignored. One might argue that the context of male offending is included in current instruments, such as the LSI-R, since these are theory based instruments, theories based on male offending. The context of female offending is left out given the lack of consideration to female offender theories (Morash, 2005). Content validity, with regard to offending, probably lies closer to the causes of offending than with correlations of offending, at least as currently measured. Predictive validity studies present correlations, and thus content and context is usually not visible. The data here are cross-sectional and getting at causes would necessitate a longitudinal design (Benda, 2005), yet the results nonetheless indicate room for theoretical concern.

While there may be overlap between what is, statistically, a criminogenic risk/need for males and females, the pathway and context of these risks/needs may, in fact, be different (Hollin & Palmer, 2006). Hollin & Palmer (2006) note that, "It is plausible that there are gender-specific pathways to offending in which adverse life events, such as abuse, become antecedents to a range of personal problems, which, in turn, lead to substance use, and so to offending." There would never be a correlation between abuse and recidivism in the LSI-R, though, both because it is not measured and, if it were, would likely be masked by the substance abuse problem (at least for females). There is recent evidence to take this dilemma seriously. The Reisig et al. (2006) study of the predictive validity of the LSI-R for a group of female offenders found that while predictive validity did exist for some of the women, it was not predictive for women whose criminal careers followed a gendered pathway as outlined by a pathways perspective on female offending. In this study, the predictive ability of the LSI-R was indeed compromised for female offenders who commit crime in this traditional female context.

The qualitative portion of this research demonstrates the need to look at the context of female offending as well, especially if one wishes to get a better picture of correlations of recidivism and, ultimately, closer to causes of (re)offending. This is particularly important if the expectation of current instruments is to also guide treatment for recidivism reduction. Context simply matters. Data presented in Chapter Four, for example, demonstrates the importance of alcohol and drug abuse with outcome, or recidivism, for female offenders. Data presented in Chapter Five demonstrates that within the context of female offending, drug and alcohol use is *directly* related to abuse, trauma, or neglect in the female offender's life. At face value this would indicate that abuse, at an aggregate level, is close to a causal factor for women's substance use and this, in turn, is linked with their offending. Attempts to treat substance abuse outside the context of its use are likely to be unsuccessful. Bloom et al. (2003, pg. 56) cite the following:

> ...a relational context is critical to success in addressing the reasons why women commit crimes, their motivations, the ways in which they change their behaviors, and their reintegration into the community. Understanding the role of

relationships and connections is thus fundamental to understanding the female offender. ... For example, women offenders who cite drug abuse as self-medication often discuss personal relationships as the cause of their pain. Abusive families and battering relationships are often strong themes in the lives of these women. This has significant implications for therapeutic interventions that deal with the impact of such relationships one women's current and future behavior.

These kinds of events both mimic what was found in the qualitative portion of this research and certainly parallel the existing theories, especially pathway, of female offending. It is fundamentally apparent from these data that abuse - sexual, physical, or emotional - marks a causal pathway into criminal offending for many women in a way that does not exist for their male counterparts. Yet, once involved in this lifestyle, the abuse per se is no longer a risk factor, or correlate of offending, but it is nonetheless an area that needs to be treated or addressed.

This is where correlation, causation, and context become problematic when counting outside of a feminist standpoint. Sprague (2005, pg. 87) notes that, historically, "...conventional methodology builds measures from the experiences of men" and, unfortunately, these methodologies have often been constructed by men who have either purposely ignored women (Hirschi, 1969) at worst or, at best, neglected to seriously consider women in their methodologies. This has resulted in the generation of facts "that legitimate privilege and even help to reproduce inequality" (Sprague, 2005; pg. 88). Ultimately, measurement is always implicated by a particular standpoint (Sprague, 2005) – either that of the researcher, the researched, or both. Failing to consider gender, both men and women, truly does a disservice to female offenders in a correctional climate now poised to positively affect recidivism via treatment rather than through purely punitive means.

In order to move beyond mere counting via correlations, we must consider causes as a matter distinct from correlations, and ones that are often implicated by the contexts within which problems occur. Failure to do so ultimately compromises content validity – even in the face of existing predictive validity. For example, many studies have already suggested a cause between childhood trauma and juvenile and adult offending for the female offender. This is especially noticeable in alcohol and drug abuse for females compared to males. Previous research on female substance abuse has been linked with physical, sexual, and emotional abuse in their lives (Widom & Hiller-Sturmhofel, 2001). In turn, substance abuse is linked with criminal offending in this and other research (Hollin & Palmer, 2006). Without questioning epistemologies about criminal (re)offending, we miss context and consequently hinder content validity.

Multiple mediating factors in female offenders' lives often mask the distinction between correlation, context, and cause. Essentially, by focusing on the prediction side, practioners have availed themselves of causal behavior and instead focus on correlations with outcome. Gilfus (2006) notes that, "substance abuse has repeatedly been found to be one of the major long term psychological effects of childhood sexual abuse." Factors like this are missed, though, when we only objectively score risks/needs based on men and skip the context of women's offending. Context is, ultimately, a mix of both cause and correlation (or risk). However, if the cause is not treated, can the risk of future offending and harm (to self and others) be positively affected?

For example, Iwilani's story demonstrates the dichotomous difficulty inherent in current risk/need assessment instruments designed for male offenders. A history of victimization may have been the cause of her initial offending and the drug abuse a later consequence. But substance abuse also correlates with risk and, thus, becomes a criminogenic need and statistically a risk for reoffending. As such, some in the criminal justice system or other helping professions might argue that this is moot – one only needs to address the problem as it currently exists. However, as with Iwilani, when she uses or abuses substances, she uses them to numb feelings that began when she was young, at the onset of her abuse. Unless the trauma related to victimization is dealt with, Iwilani and other women like her will merely turn to drugs and alcohol as a means of self-medication. Again, the neglect of gender-specific factors makes an instrument like the LSI-R a second generation for female offenders - one that is useful as a prediction tool.

Talking with the women rather than merely counting them provided the opportunity to discover *how* context matters in their lives (and men as well) as it relates to the criminal justice system. While it has been suggested that it would be too reductionist to imply that abuse alone causes criminal offending (Comack, 2006), the pattern is nonetheless too prevalent to be ignored. There is certainly no attempt here to deny that women have agency. Rather, the intent is to note that female offenders are nonetheless often constrained by context and circumstances that lead them into lives of crime (Richie, 2001).

Yet, ignoring the context of offending in female offenders' lives is certainly not a new phenomenon. Miller, in her work on female domestic violence arrests, found that (2005, pg. 1):

> ...by following the letter of the law, however, law enforcement officers often disregard the context in which victims of violence resort to using violence themselves. Often what is most revealing are the antecedents to the incident that many battered victims share: they often act in self-defense, they may have long histories of victimization at the hands of their male partners, and they may use a weapon to equalize the force or threat used by their partners, who are bigger and stronger than they are.

This is truly parallel to the situation found with women in this sample. Their initial entrée into substance abuse and drugs often *began* with victimization, albeit usually at the hands of a trusted family member.

Another example, analogous to the use of current gender-neutral instruments, is the issue of the Conflict Tactics Scale (CTS). The CTS was similarly constructed from a male standpoint of domestic violence involvement. The 'objective' application of this scale demonstrated that women and men were equally likely to be victims of domestic violence. The qualitative reality shows that the context and occurrence of domestic violence is gendered. The scale simply failed to capture the types of and circumstances surrounding the commission of domestic violence by females (Sprague, 2005).

The invisibility of the context of the victimization/offending relationship results in the treatment of male and female offenders that, at face value, appears valid but in reality proves inequitable for the female offender. Miller (2005) goes on to note that a one-size fits all approach to programming for both men and women fails to address the variation in needs for both. The same is certainly true for actuarial based risk/need instruments such as the LSI-R. The failure to admit to gender differences in offending, and the different risks and needs for both, ultimately cheats female offenders of equitable treatment and serves to continue the traditional gender neglect in criminal justice processing.

Perhaps the link between past victimization and current substance abuse dictates the need for treatment that addresses coping mechanisms rather than addiction per se (Widom and Hiller-Sturmhofel, 2001). There is a possible dual failure of the LSI-R in that it fails to moderate the right risks/needs and thus will never triage individuals (read females) into salient gender responsive programming (McDiarmid, 2005). For example, women who have sought mental health treatment for trauma, abuse, or other reasons are counted as higher risk, yet the context, the content, of that treatment for them is far from criminogenic.

Sprague (2005) reminds us that (pg. 91), "In order to guide social change, we need to understand the mechanisms that are creating the situation within which people identify their options and choose from among them." If we wish to further systems of gender inequality in the criminal justice system, and beyond, then we *should* ignore the context of female offending and continue to count salient factors of (re)offending for men as similar to those for females. However, if we are to take the true correlates of women's (re)offending seriously, we must take the time to study women from a feminist standpoint – one that considers their context of offending as different from that of men. This will help us understand their causes of (re)offending better and, ultimately, allow for policies and programs that will positively affect this subgroup of offenders. Correlation, causation, and context should not be divorced when counting or considering any social phenomenon. Further, any discussion of correlation, causation, and context should be considered within a gendered construct that understands the persistence of a gender-stratified society and how, ultimately, gender must not be forgotten in important penological issues.

Moving Forward with Risk/Need Instruments

Ultimately, readers of this book may ask a very important question. Given the findings in this and related research, should we continue to employ the use of actuarial risk/need assessment instruments, namely the LSI-R in this case, for female offenders? Is this the best way for a society to manage its offenders in terms of both surveillance and rehabilitation? The answer here is a *qualified* yes. While these and similar data indicate policy implications that center on broader sociological issues[30], the policy implications here necessarily center on current and continued use of the LSI-R as a correctional and classification tool.

It seems as if risk/need assessment instruments, at the very least, do help shape the decision making of criminal justice actors and, hence, reduce unwanted disparity in decision making. When used correctly, they will aid in public safety by identifying those who do need greater scrutiny and surveillance while serving time in the community. In turn, this could lessen the need for dependency on incarceration as punishment. However, these models need to also be as accurate as possible for the population upon which they will be applied.

We may want to use instruments like the LSI-R even if they are imperfect at informing treatment needs because of the positive impact on public safety (Bosworth, 2004; Petersilia, 2003). Others have also noted the usefulness of these instruments to the field of corrections, with the caveat that there must be a greater incorporation of theory (Gottfredson, 1987). Finally, the use of these instruments ultimately seems warranted if they help swing the pendulum back towards a rehabilitative criminal justice system (Bosworth, 2004).

Yet, there is also an issue of blind justice with these risk/need instruments. While the use of these instruments may be used to cut down on discretion, the objectivity of these instruments is nonetheless questionable when issues of gender are not considered prior to their construction. If instruments are constructed with gendered factors in mind, their utility would be in the management of discretion, risk, as well as ensuring treatment linked with rehabilitation. Again, even with error factored in, these instruments are more accurate than judgment alone and do help balance the unfettered discretion that can also result in bias in the criminal justice decision-making process (Petersilia, 2003).

Jurisdictions should therefore seriously consider whether current cutoff scores, in terms of classification levels, should be different for males and females. Given the current lack of context and attention to potentially spurious relationships, there is the danger of females being both over- and under-classified (Hollin & Palmer, 2006; Reisig et al., 2006). Research has demonstrated that, specifically, women who are

---

[30] Some of these issues and critiques are more broadly discussed following the recommendations outlined here.

socially and economically marginalized tend to be over-classified with these instruments (Reisig et al., 2006). Over-classified women may be subject to too much surveillance or be subject to services that do not meet their needs. This, in turn, may set women offenders up for failure in terms of higher revocation rates via increased surveillance and failure due to appropriate treatment.

Under-classified women, on the other hand, may be not be supervised enough and may not receive the services that they either need or that meet their needs (Reisig et al., 2006). Although the predictive validity of the instrument suggests equality, the reality, as demonstrated in this work, is that females still tend to be slightly over-classified with this instrument and hence may be subject to an unfair amount of supervision. These women may also be set up for failure via reoffending because their criminogenic needs are not met and/or they are not being adequately supervised.

Perhaps most important, though, is to create something new. In other words, it is well worth the investment to build, from the ground up, a gender-specific tool. This is especially important if one wishes to affect treatment. Again, predictive validity issues aside, if we intend to positively impact recidivism with these instruments, we must necessarily be concerned with the manner in which risk/need factors are interpreted for female versus male offenders (Belknap & Holsinger, 2006; Van Voorhis, 2005). We must also be concerned with content validity. There is, especially, a need to consider how survival strategies utilized by girls and women should be factored into these risk/need assessments (Gilfus, 2006) since the women's stories here, and elsewhere, indicate that they are indeed survivors and that any effort to help these women refrain from crime should, ideally, center on helping them continue that survivor process via pro-social mechanisms. Factors such as mental health treatment and financial assistance, in the main, should not be considered risky behavior for female offenders, even though they may be risk factors for male offenders, at an aggregate level.

Future Development and Research

There certainly exist philosophical concerns regarding the ethical and moral use of risk/need instruments in the genre of punishment. The above-mentioned recommendations stem from a more practical perspective given the current reality of the correctional system and its needs. However, there are certainly veiled costs of using actuarial risk/need assessment instruments in the administration of justice. The most important ones are outlined below.

First, the issue of whether it is just to determine levels of surveillance (which are closely aligned to issues of punishment) based on what an offender *might* do compared to what he or she *actually* did remains a contentious one (Harcourt, 2007; Hudson, 2003; Tonry, 1987). Actuarial methods ultimately provide the technology with which to make these decisions, however imprecise. Harcourt (2007, pg. 3) provides an important critique, "These technological advances are, in effect, exogenous shackles to our legal system, and this raises very troubling questions about what theory of just punishment we would independently embrace and how it is, exactly, that we have allowed technological knowledge, somewhat arbitrarily, to dictate the path of justice." Although the overall arbitrariousness of these methods is disputable[31], Harcourt nonetheless makes an important critique.

The issue of whether the criminal justice system can or should prescribe pathways through the system, including levels of punishment and treatment, based on what one might do prevents an interesting dilemma. On the one hand, the issue of treating offenders in concert with the crime committed, regardless of any other legal or extra-legal factors, appears the most appropriate way in which to deliver punishment. However, this type of criticism also runs counter to the material presented in this book. For example, women do not commit crimes, in general, in the same way or for the same reasons as do men. A society still structured around patriarchy and gender-stratification demands a decidedly gender-centered approach prior to the construction of equitable (versus equal) treatment. Further, the need to triage the highest risk offenders into treatment should necessarily balance the offender's rehabilitative needs in terms of keeping one out of the system in the future with the need to punish, and surveil, only in accordance with the crime committed. This is an area that deserves greater attention in research and the literature.

Further, the public demands risk management of the criminal justice system. The Willie Horton fiasco is a prime example of the

---

[31] Refer back to Chapter Two regarding the creation and history of these instruments.

public's outrage when a potential risk has not been managed according to some identifiable (real or perceived) standard. While this is often an unfair criticism, it is a problematic area nonetheless. Ultimately, though, "the risk to the public of being victimized must be balanced against the risk to offenders (actual and potential) of undermined restriction of liberty and other factors of deprivation" (Hudson, 2003; pg. 46). This is, perhaps, the largest unresolved issue stemming from the use of actuarial methods. This seems especially crucial, currently, for female offenders. This research does not resolve this balance – but it is nonetheless an important area for future research and policy development.

Secondly, one must consider how financial concerns play into the construction and application of these actuarial instruments. It has been stated that with mass incarceration came the prison industrial complex. More realistically, the use of risk/need instruments is very much a part of this correctional industrial complex. Business certainly extends beyond institutional bars and touches community correctional populations as well. Actuarial risk/need instruments are a large part of this business and have been adopted as one cost-effective way in which to deliver ever more scarce resources to a continually growing correctional population. How much of a part of the business side of corrections this represents is unknown, but the truth remains that these instruments, typically, are proprietary and include a cost per usage fee. However, we need to be cautious not to overlook this important aspect. Harcourt notes (2007, pg. 188), "Profiling has become second nature because of our natural tendency to favor economic efficiency."

Organizations are able to incorporate these instruments readily because, in the main, they are adopted to solve capacity problems. For probation and parole, this means too many offenders to supervise in the community and not enough recourses (officers, programs, or otherwise) to adequately do so. While the effort to include an actuarial risk/need instrument that purports to incorporate treatment back into corrections is an important ideological concept, a genuine concern is that their use may also become a method of convenience without the conscious at some point. In other words, if not managed properly, these instruments, all good intentions aside, could end up punishing more, not less. Harcourt's (2007) argument with regard to this topic might be that rather than the achievement of a net reduction in recidivism via targeting those most likely to recidivate, we will ultimately *increase* recidivism if the targeted population is not amenable to change and the 'left alone' population continues to offend. Thus far, however, this pattern is challenged by the evidence on the risk principle (see again Chapter Two).

Third, and in line with what this research has outlined, is the idea that the nature of a control versus treatment philosophy is at odds in these instruments. This research has suggested that the current instruments may well be working as third generation instruments for male offenders but as only second generation ones for female offenders. As such, this ultimately means that men get treatment while women get control. The potential for problematic processes and outcomes are possible when we rely too heavily on actuarial methods to guide our philosophical foundations for punishment, treatment, or both. Hudson (2003, pg. 48) notes the following, "These new risk strategies are not, then, making clinical judgments that a particular offender is likely to reoffend, but actuarial judgments that this person possesses the characteristics associated with reoffending." There needs to be a mechanism in place that allows for both – a realistic mechanism for control coupled with a genuine allowance for that treatment philosophy. Fourth, and in line with what has been mentioned above, is a concern with 'counting' women's prior abuse histories as risk factors or criminogenic needs. Since there is a link between past histories of abuse and offending, either current or onset, considering abuse in any standardized manner may, in fact, serve to further penalize the female offender. This poses an interesting dilemma surrounding the continued use of these instruments. While the histories of abuse should be considered when contemplating the treatment needs of female offenders, possible punishment for that abuse is unwarranted. In the end, there needs to be a system that recognizes the disproportionate histories of abuse faced by female offenders while not overly controlling them for factors that are, or were, beyond their control (Tonry, 1987). Otherwise these instruments may become the veil behind which we continue to disadvantage female offenders, namely by treating them as 'objectively' similar to males. The instruments may "accentuate the prejudices and biases that are built into the penal code" (Harcourt, 2007; pg. 190), or, in this case, into the use of currently constructed actuarial risk/need instruments.

Fifth, while it is argued here and elsewhere that these instruments may in fact reduce disparity in correctional decision-making and may improve public safety by treating offenders in the community and keeping them out of prison, it should also be noted that one recent scholar makes a compelling case that challenges this assumption. Harcourt (2007) argues that the reliance on actuarial methods produces what he calls a ratchet effect. In sum, the ratchet effect refers to the process whereby we disproportionately focus on a perceived high rate offending group, and continue to re-shape and focus our resources on this group. What happens, then, is that the prison population is not a reflection of the true offender population, but a disproportionate reflection of the targeted population. This, in turn, according to Harcourt, might possibly increase crime if the targeted group is not responsive to the increased security and the non-targeted groups are allowed to continue to commit crime in an undeterred fashion. While Harcourt is mainly discussing the role of actuarial methods in policing, there exists a connection to this research. While his is a new critique in this area, and runs counter to many current claims, the issues are important and demand further attention as this salient area of corrections continues to develop.

Further, it is unknown whether the officers that administer these instruments also interpret the offender response too superficially because they are looking at individual responses and not at gendered patterns of offending and reoffending. In other words, these actuarial risk/need instruments are based on what we know about offending at aggregate levels for men, yet we apply them to individuals (including women). We should consider concerns of ecological fallacies. In other words, do we understand individuals solely based on their objective scores to these instruments? Certainly the large scale incorporation of these instruments also shapes the way that criminal justice practioners think about criminality in terms of risks and needs rather than on individual behavior.

However, for men as well as for women, context is ever important. It is worth researching whether individual probation and parole officer interactions with offenders under their supervision are fully affected by the offender's membership with his or her aggregate group or within the context of his or her individual situation, or both. The issue of ecological fallacy seems more prevalent for females, though, considering the research outlined in this book. If epistemological issues of both male/female offending were considered, we would know that, regardless of the type of answer, women often represent something different when it comes to alcohol and substance abuse, relationships, treatment, and other indicators. More work is needed to assess the practical and ethical implications of these instruments for females specifically and all offenders generally.

Finally, there is a need to ultimately look beyond the predictive and content validity and determine how well the instrument works as fully intended. In other words, does the LSI-R effectively aid in case management and rehabilitation for *both* female and male offenders? The recent Reisig et al. study (2006) would suggest that this is not the case may not be the case.

The cautions outlined herein certainly seem, at face value, to conflict with my recommendations to maintain the use of these instruments. My recommendations to continue with their usage comes from a very realistic fear that throwing the baby out with the bathwater, so to speak, will also mean that the renewed attention to rehabilitation will go down the drain as well. However, the biggest benefit to their maintenance in the contemporary criminal justice landscape centers on their allowance for very real discussions of rehabilitation as well as evidence-based treatment programs designed to keep offenders out of the system rather than as a mechanism to keep them in the system for increasingly longer and harsher periods of time.

In the end, more research needs to be conducted on both the professional use of these instruments, the theory or lack thereof behind them (Gottfredson, 1987), and their ultimate utility in the criminal justice system overall. Measurement in future research should employ targeted attempts to include both operationalizations and conceptualizations that include what is known about female offending (Reisig et al., 2006, Hannah-Moffat & Shaw, 2003; Olsen et al., 2003).

Finally, the philosophical caveats outlined above should be seriously explored in the future by scholars and practitioners alike. Efficacy of correctional practices is not the only factor that should be considered in the application of protocols to offenders. Greater discussion around the meaning of control, treatment, cost, and just punishment should follow future discussions centered on the continued use of actuarial risk/need assessment instruments. Included here should be future research and dialogue on how much, if at all, these actuarial risk/need instruments are really saving jurisdictions, if at all. What are their overall costs – both economic and social? Important as well is future research that centers on the following important question:

Re-Considering Female Offenders – Context Matters

How do we create a just risk/need assessment instrument that does not penalize women for past victimization yet also allows for the context of that victimization to be included, legally and ethically, in a manner that best *helps* offenders – both female and male – as well as improves public safety? In fact, future work needs to attempt to fuse the practical side the usage of these instruments with the very important philosophical, moral, and ethical side. The recent Reisig et al. (2006) and Harcourt (2007) works, as well as material presented in this book, present a good starting point.

References

Anderson, Elijah. 1999. *Code of the Street: Decency, Violence, and the Moral Life of the Inner City.* New York, NY: W. W. Norton & Company.

Andrews, D.A., Jerry J. Kiessling, David Robinson, and Susan Mickus. 1989. "The Risk Principle of Case Classification: An Outcome Evaluation with Young Adult Probationers." *Canadian Journal of Criminology* 28:377-384.

Andrews, D. A., James Bonta, and R. D. Hoge. 1990. "Classification for Effective Rehabilitation: Rediscovering Psychology." *Criminal Justice and Behavior* 17:19-52.

Andrews, D.A. and James L. Bonta. 2000. *The Level of Service Inventory-Revised: User's Manual.* Canada: Multi-Health Systems.

Austin, J. 2003. *Findings in Prison Classification and Risk Assessment.* National Institute of Corrections.

Austin, James, Dana Coleman, Johnette Peyton, and Kelly Dedel Johnson. 2003. *Reliability and Validity Study of the LSI-R Risk Assessment Instrument, Final Report Submitted to the Pennsylvania Board of Probation and Parole.* Available at the Web site of the Pennsylvania Commission on Crime and Delinquency, Center for Research, Evaluation, and Statistical Analysis: http://www.pccd.state.pa.us/pccd/cwp/view.asp?A51390&Q5574731.

Baird, Christopher. 2009. *A Question of Evidence: A Critique of Risk Assessment Models Used in the Justice System.* National Council on Crime and Delinquency.

Belknap, Joanne. 2007. *The Invisible Woman: Gender, Crime, and Justice (3rd edition).* Belmont, CA: Thomson.

Belknap, Joanne, and Kristi Holsinger. 2006. "The Gendered Nature of Risk Factors for Delinquency." *Feminist Criminology* 1: 48-71.

Benda, Brent B. 2005. "Gender Differences in Life-Course Theory of Recidivism: A Survival Analysis." *International Journal of*

Offender Therapy and Comparative Criminology 49: 325-342.

Blanchette, Kelly. 2004. "Re-Designing Corrections for Women: The Canadian Experience." *Journal of Community Corrections* 13:11-22.

Blanchette, Kelley and Shelley L. Brown. 2006. *The Assessment and Treatment of Women Offenders: An Integrative Perspective.* Hoboken, NJ: John Wiley & Sons, Ltd.

Bloom, Barbara. 2000. "Gender-Responsive Supervision and Programming for Women Offenders in the Community." *Responding to Women Offenders in the Community.* Topics in Community Corrections Annual Issue.

Bloom, Barbara and Barbara Owen. 2002. *Gender-Responsive Strategies: Research, Practice, and Guiding Principles for Women Offenders.* National Institute of Corrections.

Bloom, Barbara, Barbara Owen and Stephanie Covington. 2003. *Gender-Responsive Strategies: Research, Practice, and Guiding Principles for Women Offenders.* National Institute of Corrections, U.S. Department of Justice.

Bonta, James. 1989. "Native Inmates: Institutional Response, Risk, and Needs." *Canadian Journal of Criminology* 39:49-62.

Bonta, James and Laurence L. Motiuk. 1992. "Inmate Classification." *Journal of Criminal Justice* 20:343-353.

Bonta, James, Bessie Pang, and Suzanne Wallace-Carpetta. 1995. "Predictors of Recidivism Among Incarcerated Female Offenders." *The Prison Journal* 75:277-294.

Bonta, James. 1996. "Risk-Needs Assessment and Treatment." In *Choosing Correctional Options that Work: Defining the Demand and Evaluating the Supply,* ed. Alan T. Harland. Thousand Oaks: Sage Publications.

Bonta, James, Brad Bogue, Michael Crowley and Laurence Motiuk. 2001. "Implementing Offender Classification Systems: Lessons Learned" In *Offender Rehabilitation in Practice: Implementing and Evaluating Effective Programs,* ed. Gary A. Bernfeld, David P. Farrington and Alan W. Leschied. Hoboken, NJ: John Wiley & Sons.

Bonta, James. 2002. "Offender Risk Assessment: Guidelines for Selection and Use." *Criminal Justice & Behavior* 29:355-379.

Bosworth, Mary. 2004. Editorial Introduction: Gender, Risk, and Recidivism." *Criminology and Public Policy* 3:181-184.

Bourgois, Philippe. 2003. *In Search of Respect: Selling Crack in El*

Barrio. New York, NY: Cambridge University Press.
Brennan, Tim. 1998. "Institutional Classification of Females: Problems and Some Proposals for Reform." In *Female Offenders: Critical Perspectives & Effective Interventions,* ed. Ruth T. Zaplin. Gaithersburg, MD: Aspen Publishing.
Brumbaugh, Susan and Danielle M. Steffey. 2005. "The Importance of Constructing and Validating Risk Assessment Instruments in Community Corrections Settings." *Justice Research and Policy* 7:57-83.
Champion, Dean J. 1994. *Measuring Offender Risk: A Criminal Justice Sourcebook.* Santa Barbara, CA: Greenwood Press.
Chesney-Lind, Meda. 1997. *The Female Offender: Girls, Women and Crime.* Thousand Oaks: Sage Publications.
Chesney-Lind, Meda. 1998. "Foreword." In *Female Offenders: Critical Perspectives and Effective Interventions,* ed. Ruth T. Zaplin. Gaithersburg: Aspen Publishers, Inc.
Chesney-Lind, Meda. 2000. "Women and the Criminal Justice System: Gender Matters." *In Responding to Women Offenders in the Community.* Topics in Community Corrections Annual Issue.
Chesney-Lind, Meda. 2002. "Imprisoning Women: The Unintended Victims of Mass Imprisonment." In *Invisible Punishment: The Collateral Consequences of Mass Imprisonment,* ed. Marc Mauer and Meda-Chesney-Lind. New York: The New Press.
Chesney-Lind, Meda and Lisa Pasko. 2004. *The Female Offender: Girls, women, and crime.* Thousand Oaks, CA: Sage.
Chesney-Lind, Meda. 2006. "Patriarchy, Crime, and Justice: Feminist Backlash in an Era of Backlash." *Feminist Criminology* 1: 6-26.
Chia, Louise. *Risk Assessment and Level of Service – Using the Level of Service Inventory-Revised (LSI-R).* 2000. Paper presented at the 2000 Probation and Community Correction Officers Association, Australia.
Clear, Todd R. 2003. "Inmate Classification – Editorial Introduction." *Criminology and Public Policy* 2: 213-214.
Clements, Carl.B. 1996. "Offender Classification: Two Decades of Progress." *Criminal Justice and Behavior* 23:121-143.
Comack, Elizabeth. 2006. "Coping, Resisting, and Surviving: Connecting Women's Law Violations to Their Histories of Abuse."

In *In Her Own Words: Women Offenders' Views on Crime and Victimization,* ed. Leanne Fiftal Alarid and Paul Cromwell. Los Angeles: Roxbury Publishing Company.

Covington, Stephanie S. and Barbara E. Bloom. 2003. "Gendered Justice: Women in the Criminal Justice System." In *Gendered Justice: Addressing Female Offenders,* ed. Barbara E. Bloom. Durham, NC: Carolina Academic Press.

Coulson, Grant, Giorgio Ilacqua, Verna Nutbrown, Diana Giulekas, and Francis Cudjoe. 1996. "Predictive Utility of the LSI for Incarcerated Female Offenders." *Criminal Justice and Behavior* 23:427-439.

Daly, Kathleen. 1984. *Gender, Crime, and Punishment.* New Haven:Yale University Press.

Daly, Kathleen and Meda Chesney-Lind. "Feminism and Criminology." *Justice Quarterly* 5:497-538.

Deschenes, Elizabeth P., Barbara Owen, and Jason Crow. 2006. *Recidivism among Female Prisoners: Secondary Analysis of the 1994 BJS Recidivism Data Set.* Bureau of Justice Statistics. U.S. Department of Justice.

Ditton, Paula M. 1999. *Mental Health and Treatment of Inmates and Probationers.* Bureau of Justice Statistics. U.S. Department of Justice.

Dowden, Craig, and D.A. Andrews. 1999. "What Works for Female Offenders: A Meta-Analytic Review." *Journal of Crime & Delinquency* 45:438-452.

Fagan, Abigail A., M.L. Van Horn, David J. Hawkins, and Michael W. Arthur. 2007. "Gender Similarities and Differences in the Association Between Risk and Protective Factors and Self-Reported Serious Delinquency." *Prevention Science* 8:115-124.

Farr, Kathryn Ann. 2000. "Classification for Female Inmates: Moving Forward." *Crime and Delinquency* 46: 3-17.

Farrington, David P. and Roger Tarling. 1985. "Criminological Prediction: An Introduction in Prediction in Criminology". In *Prediction in Criminology,* ed. David P. Farrington and Roger Tarling. Ablany, NY: State University of New York Press.

Farrington, David P. and Kate A. Painter. 2004. *Gender Differences in Offending: Implications for Risk-Focused Prevention.* Home Office Online Repot 09/04.

References

Federal Bureau of Investigation. 2008. *Crime in the United States, 2007.* Federal Bureau of Investigation. U.S. Department of Justice.

Feely, Malcolm M. and Jonathan Simon. 1992. "The New Penology: Notes on the Emerging Study of Corrections and Its Implications." *Criminology* 30:449-475.

Ferraro, Kathleen J. and Angela M. Moe. 2006. "Criminalized Mothers: The Value and Devaluation of Parenthood from Behind Bars." *Women & Therapy* 29:135-164.

Flavin, Jeanne. 2004. "Employment Counseling, Housing Assistance...and Aunt Yolanda?: How Strengthening Families' Social Capital Can Reduce Recidivism." *Criminology and Public Policy* 3:209-216.

Flavin, Jeanne and Amy Desautels. 2006. "Feminism and Crime." In *Rethinking Gender, Crime and Justice: Feminist Readings,* Ed. Claire M. Renzetti, Lynne Goodstein, and Susan L. Miller. Los Angeles, CA: Roxbury Publishing Company.

Flowers, R. Barri. 2003, *Male Crime and Deviance: Exploring Its Causes, Dynamic, and Nature.* Springfield, IL: Thomas Books.

Foucault, Michel. 1977. *Discipline and Punish: The Birth of the Prison.* New York: Vintage Books.

Funk, Stephanie, J. 1999. "Risk Assessment for Juveniles on Probation: A Focus on Gender." *Criminal Justice and Behavior* 26:44-68.

Gelsthorpe, Loraine. 2004. "Female Offending: A Theoretical Overview." In *Women Who Offend,* ed. Gill McIvor. New York: Jessica Kingsley Publishers Ltd.

Gilfus, Mary E. 2006. "From Victims to Survivors to Offenders." In *Her Own Words: Women Offenders' Views on Crime and Victimization,* ed. Leanne Fiftal Alarid and Paul Cromwell. Los Angeles, CA: Roxbury Publishing Company.

Glaze, Lauren E. and Thomas P. Bonczar. 2007. *Probation and Parole in the United States, 2006.* Bureau of Justice Statistics. U.S. Department of Justice.

Goertzel, Ted. 2002. "Myths of Murder and Multiple Regression." *The Skeptical Enquirer* 26: 19-23.

Gottfredson, Don M. 1987. "Prediction and Classification in Criminal Justice Decision Making." In *Prediction and Classification:*

Criminal Justice Decision Making, ed. Don M. Gottfredson and Michael Tonry. Chicago: University of Chicago press.

Gottfredson, Don M. and Howard N. Snyder. 2005. *The Mathematics of Risk Classification: Changing Data into Valid Instruments for Juvenile Courts.* National Center for Juvenile Justice.

Gottfredson, Michael R. 2005. "Offender Classifications and Treatment Effects in Development Criminology: A Propensity/Event Consideration." *The Annals of the American Academy* 602:46-56.

Gottfredson, Stephen D., and Don M. Gottfredson. 1985. "Screening for Risk among Parolees: Policy, Practice, and Method." In *Prediction in Criminology,* ed. David P. Farrington and Roger Tarling. Ablany, NY: State University of New York Press.

Gottfredson, Stephen D. 1987. "Statistical and Actuarial Considerations." In *The Prediction of Criminal Violence,* ed. Fernand N. Dutile and Cleon H. Foust. Springfield, Illinois: Charles C. Thomas Publisher.

Gottfredson, Don M. and Howard N. Snyder. 2005. *The Mathematics of Risk Classification: Changing Data into Valid Instruments for Juvenile Courts.* National Center for Juvenile Justice.

Hagedorn, John M. 1998. "Frat Boys, Bossmen, Studs, and Gentlemen: a Typology of Gang Masculinities." In *Masculinities and Violence: Research on Men and Masculinities,* ed. Lee H. Bowker. Thousand Oaks, CA: Sage Publications.

Hannah-Moffat, Kelly and Margaret Shaw. 2001. *Taking Risks: Incorporating Gender and Culture into the Classification and Assessment of Federally Sentenced Women in Canada.* Status of Women Canada.

Hannah-Moffit, Kelly and Margaret Shaw. 2003. "The Meaning of 'Risk' in Women's Prisons: A Critique." In *Gendered Justice: Addressing Female Offenders,* ed. Barbara Bloom. Durham, NC: Carolina Academic Press.

Hannah-Moffat, Kelly. 2009. "Gridlock or mutability: Reconsidering "gender" and risk Assessment." *Criminology & Public Policy,* 8:209-219.

Harcourt, Bernard E. 2007. *Against prediction: Profiling, Policing, and Punishing in an Actuarial Age.* Chicago: University of Chicago Press.

Harer, Miles D. and Neal P. Langan. 2001. "Gender Differences in

Predictors of Prison Violence: Assessing the Predictive Validity of a Risk Classification System." *Crime & Delinquency* 47: 513-536.

Harlow, Caroline Wolf. 1999. *Prior Abuse Reported by Inmates and Probationers*. Bureau of Justice Statistics. U.S. Department of Justice.

Heilbrun, Kirk, David DeMatteo, Ralph Fretz, Jacey Erickson, Kento Yasuhara, and Natalie Anumba. 2008. "How "Specific" Are Gender-Specific Rehabilitation Needs?" *Criminal Justice and Behavior* 35:1382-1397.

Hirschi, Travis. 1969. *Causes of Delinquency*. Berkeley, CA: University of California Press.

Hollin, Clive R. and Emma J. Palmer. 2006. "Criminogenic need and women offenders: A critique of the literature." *Legal and Criminological Psychology* 11:179-195.

Holtfreter, Kristy, Michael D. Reisig, and Merry Morash. 2004. "Poverty, State Capital, and Recidivism Among Women Offenders." *Criminology and Public Policy* 3:185-208.

Holtfreter, Kristy and Rhonda Cupp. 2007. "Gender and Risk Assessment: The Empirical Status of the LSI-R for Women." *Journal of Contemporary Criminal Justice* 23:363-382.

Holsinger, Alexander M., Author J. Lurigio, J., and Edward J. Latessa. 2001. "Practitioners' Guide to Understanding the Basis of Assessing Offender Risk." *Federal Probation* 65: 46-50.

Holsinger, Alexander M. and Edward J. Latessa. 2003. "Ethnicity, gender, and the Level of Service Inventory-Revised." *Journal of Criminal Justice* 31: 309-320.

Holsinger, Kristi and Patricia Van Voorhis. 2005. "Examining Gender Inequities in Classification Systems: Missouri's Development of a Gender-Responsive Assessment Instrument." *Women Girls & Criminal Justice* 6:33-48.

Hubbard, Dana Jones and Travis C. Pratt. 2004. "The Criminogenic Needs of Girls: What are the Most Important Risk Factors for Delinquency and Are They Different from the Risk Factors for Boys?" *Women, Girls, and Criminal Justice*. August/September 2004: 57-63.

Hubbard, Dana Jones and Betsy Matthews. 2008. "Reconciling the Differences Between the "Gender-Responsive" and the "What Works" Literature to Improve Services for Girls." *Crime &*

Delinquency 54:225-258.

Hudson, Barbara. 2003. *Justice in the Risk Society: Challenging and Re-Affirming Justice in Late Modernity*. Thousand Oaks, CA: Sage Publications.

James, Dorris J. 2004. *Profile of Jail Inmates, 2002*. Bureau of Justice Statistics. U.S. Department of Justice.

Jones, Dana A. 1999. "Case Classification in Community Corrections: Preliminary Findings from a National Survey." *Topics in Community Corrections*. National Institute of Corrections. U.S. Department of Justice.

Jones, Peter R. 1996. "Risk Prediction in Criminal Justice." In *Choosing Correctional Options that Work: Defining the Demand and Evaluating the Supply*, ed. Alan T. Harland. Thousand Oaks, CA: Sage Publications.

Jones, Stephen. 2006. *Criminology*. Oxford: Oxford University Press.

Kruttschnitt, Candace and Rosemary Gartner. 2003. "Women's Imprisonment." *Crime and Justice: A Review of Research* 30:1-82.

Langan, Patrick A., and David J. Levin. 2002. *Recidivism of Prisoners Released in 1994*. Bureau of Justice Statistics. U.S. Department of Justice.

Latessa, Edward J., 1999. "Classifying and Assessing Offenders: Understanding the Criminal Mind." *Corrections Today* 61: 8-10.

Lawrence, Sharmila, Michelle Chau and Mary Clare Lennon. 2004. *Depression, Substance Abuse, and Domestic Violence*. National Center for Children in Poverty. Columbia University Mailman School of Public Health.

Loader, Ian and Richard Sparks. 2002. "Contemporary Landscapes of Crime, Order, and Control: Governance, Risk, and Globalization." In *The Oxford Handbook of Criminology*, ed. Mike Maguire, Rod Morgan, and Robert Reiner. Oxford: Oxford University Press.

Lowenkamp, Christopher L., Alexander M. Holsinger, and Edward J. Latessa. 2001. "Risk/Need Assessment, Offender Classification, and the Role of Childhood Abuse." *Criminal Justice and Behavior* 28:543-563.

Lowenkamp, Christopher L. and Edward J. Latessa 2004. "Empirical Evidence on the Importance of Training and Experience in Using the Level of Service Inventory – Revised." *Topics in Community Corrections: Assessment Issues for Managers*. National Institute of Justice. U.S. Department of Justice.

References

Lynch, Mary. 2000. "Rehabilitation as rhetoric." *Punishment & Society* 2: 40-65.

Manchak, Sarah M., Jennifer L. Skeem, Kevin S. Douglas, and Maro Siranosian. 2009. "Does Gender Moderate the Predictive Utility of the Level of Service Inventory Revised (LSI-R) for Serious Violent Offenders?" *Criminal Justice and Behavior* 36:425-442.

Mauer, Marc and Meda Chesney-Lind. 2002. "Introduction." In *Invisible Punishment: The Collateral Consequences of Mass Imprisonment*, ed. Marc Mauer and Meda Chesney-Lind. New York: The New Press.

Maurutto, Paula and Kelly Hannah-Moffat. 2007. "Response to Commentary: Cross-Examining Risk "Knowledge." *Canadian Journal of Criminology and Criminal Justice* 49:543-550.

McDiarmid, Anne. *Gender Responsivity*. Presentation to the Hawaii Department of Public Safety, July 11, 2005.

McLvor, Gill, Cathy Murray and Janet Jamieson. 2004. "Desistance from crime: is it different for women and girls?" In *After Crime and Punishment: Pathways to Offender Reintegration*, ed. Shadd Maruna and Russ Immarigeon. Portland, OR: William Publishing.

McMahon, Maeve. 2000. "Assisting Female Offenders: Art or Science? – Chairperson's Commentary." *Assessment to Assistance: Programs for Women in Community Corrections*. International Community Corrections Association Conference.

Messerschmidt, James W. 2000. *Nine Lives: Adolescent Masculinities, the Body, and Violence*. Boulder, CO: Westview Press.

Miller, Jody. 2004. "Feminist Theories of Women's Crime: Robbery as a Case Study." In *The Criminal Justice System and Women: Offenders, Prisoners, Victims, and Workers*, ed. Barbara Raffel Price and Natalie J. Sokoloff. Columbus, OH: McGraw Hill.

Miller, Susan L. 2005. *Victims as Offenders: The Paradox of Women's Violence in Relationships*. New Brunswick: Rutgers University Press.

Modley, Phyllis. 2000. "Foreword." *Responding to Women Offenders in the Community*. Topics in Community Corrections Annual Issue. National Institute of Justice. U.S. Department of Justice.

Morash, Merry, Timothy S. Bynum, and Barbara A. Koons. 1998. *Women Offenders: Programming Needs and Promising Approaches*. Research in Brief. National Institute of Justice. U.S. Department of Justice.

Morash, Merry. 1999. "A Consideration of Gender in Relation to Social Learning and Social Structure: A General Theory of Crime and Deviance." *Theoretical Criminology* 3:451-461.

Morash, Merry 2005. *Understanding Gender, Crime, and Justice*. Thousand Oaks, CA: Sage Publications.

Morash, Merry. 2009. "A great debate over using the Level of Service Inventory-Revised (LSI-R) with women offenders." *Criminology & Public Policy* 8:173-181.

Motiuk, Laurence, James Bonta, and Don A. Andrews. 1986. "Classification in correctional halfway houses the relative and incremental predictive criterion validities of the Megargee-MMPI and LSI systems." *Criminal Justice and Behavior* 13: 33-46.

Mumola, Christopher J. 2000. *Incarcerated Parents and Their Children*. Bureau of Justice Statistics Special Report. U.S. Department of Justice.

Olson, David E., Megan Alderden, and Arthur J. Lurigio. 2003. "Men are from Mars, Women are from Venus, but what Role Does Gender Play in Probation Recidivism?" *Journal of the Justice Research and Statistics Association* 5:33-54.

Owen, Barbara. 1998. *In the Mix: Struggle and Survival in a Women's Prison*. New York: State University of New York Press.

Owen, Barbara. 2003. "Differences with a Distinction: Women Offenders and Criminal Justice Practice." In *Gendered Justice: Addressing Female Offenders,* ed. Barbara E. Bloom. Durham, NC: Carolina Academic Press.

Parsons, Mickey L., and Carmen Warner Robbins. 2002. "Factors that Support Women's Successful Transition to the Community Following Jail/Prison." *Heath Care for Women International* 23:6-18.

Petersilia, Joan. 2003. *When Prisoners Come Home: Parole and Prisoner Reentry*. Oxford: Oxford University Press.

Price, Ronald. 1997. "On the risks of risk prediction." *The Journal of Forensic Psychiatry* 8:1-4.

Raynor, Peter. 2007. "Risk and Need Assessment in British Probation: The Contribution of LSI-R." *Psychology, Crime & Law* 13:125-138.

Reisig, Michael D., Kristy Holtfreter and Merry Morash. 2006. "Assessing Recidivism Across Female Pathways to Crime." *Justice Quarterly* 23: 384-405.

Richards, Stephen C. and Jeffrey Ian Ross. 2003. "A Convict Perspective on the Classification of Prisoners." *Criminology and Public Policy* 2:243-252.

Richie, Beth E. 2001. "Challenges Incarcerated Women Face as They Return to Their Communities: Findings From Life History Interviews." *Crime & Delinquency* 47: 368-389.

Sabol, William J. and Todd D. Minton. 2008. *Jail Inmates at Midyear 2007*. Bureau of Justice Statistics. U.S. Department of Justice.

Sabol, William J. and Heather Couture. 2008. *Prison Inmates at Midyear 2007*. Bureau of Justice Statistics. U.S. Department of Justice.

Sampson, Robert J. and John H. Laub. 2005. "A Life-Course View of the Development of Crime." *The Annals of the American Academy of Political and Social Sciences* 602:12-45.

Severson, Margaret and Christian Wilson Duclos. 2005. *American Indian Suicides in Jail: Can Risk Screening Culturally Sensitive?* National Institute of Justice. U.S. Department of Justice.

Simon, Jonathan. 1993. *Poor Discipline: Control of the Underclass*. Chicago: University of Chicago Press.

Singleton, Royce A., Bruce C. Straits, and Margaret Miller Straits. 1993. Approaches to Social Research. New York: Oxford University Press.

Smith, David J. 2002. "Crime and the Life Course." In *The Oxford Handbook of Criminology,* ed. Mike McGuire, Rob Morgan, and Robert Reiner. Oxford: Oxford University Press.

Smith, Paula, Francis T. Cullen, and Edward J. Latessa. 2009. "Can 14,737 women be wrong? A meta-analysis of the LSI-R and recidivism for female offenders." *Criminology & Public Policy* 8:183-208.

Snell, Tracy L. 2006. *Capital Punishment, 2005*. Bureau of Justice Statistics. U.S. Department of Justice.

Sommers, Ira, Deborah R. Baskin and Jeffrey Fagan. 2006. "Pathways Out of Crime: Crime Desistance by Female Street Offenders." In

In Her Own Words: Women Offenders' Views on Crime and Victimization, ed. Leanne Fiftal Alarid and Paul Cromwell. Los Angeles, CA: Roxbury Publishing Company.

Sprague, Joe. 2005. *Feminist Methodologies for Critical Researchers: Bridging Differences.* Walnut Creek, CA: AltaMira Press.

Stuart, Bryan and Janet Brice-Baker. 2004. "Correlates of higher rates of recidivism in female prisoners: an exploratory study." *The Journal of Psychiatry and Law* 32: 29-70.

Taylor, Kelly N. and Kelly Blanchette. 2009. "The women are not wrong: It is the approach that is debatable." *Criminology & Public Policy* 8:221-229.

Tonry, Michael. 1987. *Prediction and Classification: Legal and Ethical Issues,* ed. Don M. Gottfredson and Michael Tonry. Chicago: University of Chicago Press.

Tonry, Michael and Joan Petersilia. 1999. *Prison Research at the Beginning of the 21st Century.* National Institute of Justice. U.S. Department of Justice.

Van Voorhis, Patricia and Lois Presser. 2001. *Classification of Women Offenders: A National Assessment of Current Practices.* National Institute of Corrections. U.S. Department of Justice.

Van Voorhis, Patricia. 2005. *Gender Responsive Assessments.* Presentation Given in Honolulu, Hawaii at the Department of Public Safety on July 11, 2005.

Van Voorhis, Patricia, Emily Salisbury, Emily Wright, and Ashley Bauman. 2008. *Achieving Accurate Pictures of Risk and Identifying Gender Responsive Needs: Two New Assessments for Women Offenders.* National Institute of Corrections. U.S. Department of Justice.

Veysey, Bonita M. and Zachary Hamilton. 2007. "Girls Will Be Girls: Gender Differences in Predictors of Success for Diverted Youth with Mental Health and Substance Abuse Disorders." *Journal of Contemporary Criminal Justice* 23:341-362.

Vose, Brenda, Frances T. Cullen, and Paula Smith. 2008. "The Empirical Status of the Level of Service Inventory." *Federal Probation* 72:22-29.

Warren, Jennifer. 2008. *One in 100: Behind Bars in America 2008.* Pew Center on the States and Public Safety Performance Project. Available at: www.pewcenteronthestates.org.

West, Heather C. and William J. Sabol. 2008. *Prisoners in 2007.*

Bureau of Justice Statistics. U.S. Department of Justice.
Whitaker, Mary Scully. 2000. "Responding to Women Offenders: Equitable Does Not Mean Identical." *Responding to Women Offenders in the Community*. NIC Topics in Community Corrections Annual Issue. National Institute of Corrections. U.S. Department of Justice.
Widom, Cathy S. 1995. *Victims of Childhood Sexual Abuse – Later Criminal Consequences*. National Institute of Justice. U.S. Department of Justice.
Widom, Cathy Spatz and Michael G. Maxfield. 2001. *An Update on the "Cycle of Violence."* National Institute of Justice. U.S. Department of Justice.
Widom, Cathy Spatz and Susanne Hiller-Sturmhofel. 2001. "Alcohol Abuse as Risk Factor for and Consequence of Child Abuse." *Alcohol Research and Health* 25:52-57.
Wright, Jen. 2002. "Next Step: Creating Gender Responsive Risk Assessment Tools." *Women, Girls & Criminal Justice* 3:81-94.
Zamble, Edward and Vernon L. Quinsey. 2001. *The Criminal Recidivism Process*. New York, NY: Cambridge University Press.

INDEX

Actuarial justice, problems with, 22
Actuarial risk instruments,
   Accuracy of, 26-27
   Bruce, 25
   Burgess, 25
   clinical judgment, 23, 26
   definition, 13, 19
   description of, 19-21
   first-generation, 25
   gender-neutral, 3
   Ohlin, 25
   reliance upon, 13, 18-19
   risk management, 17
   risk versus need, 20-21
   second-generation, 25-26
   third-generation, 28
Alderden, Megan, 4, 7, 14, 34, 35-37, 39, 41, 57, 109
Anderson, Elijah, 8, 9
Andrews, Don A., 14, 26, 32, 34, 45, 74, 119, 125, 139, 142
Anumba, Natalie, 30-31, 40
Arthur, Michael W., 27, 37, 57
Austin, James, 20, 61
Baird, Christopher, 19-20, 35, 54, 159
Baskin, Deborah R., 4, 7, 49, 66, 73
Bauman, Ashley, 4, 9-10, 14, 26, 27, 29-31, 36-37, 40-41, 82, 162
Belknap, Joanne, 1, 3-5, 7, 9, 10-12, 14, 34, 51, 52-53, 61, 125, 126, 144, 149, 171
Benda, Brent B., 31, 52, 164
Blanchette, Kelly, 13-14, 23-24, 31, 41-42, 47, 116, 119, 121, 125, 133, 139, 153, 159, 162
Bloom, Barbara, 4, 6-7, 9-12, 29-31, 33-34, 37, 41, 43-44, 52, 61, 70-71, 161, 165
Bonta, James L., 19, 23, 25-27, 32-34, 36, 42, 45, 74, 119, 125, 139, 142
Bonczar, Thomas P., 4, 12, 18
Bosworth, Mary, 19, 22, 24, 27, 36, 169, 171
Bourgois, Philippe, 8
Brennan, Tim, 41, 56
Brice-Baker, Janet, 13, 29
Brown, Shelley L., 13-14, 23-24, 41, 47, 116, 119, 121, 125, 133, 139, 153, 159, 162
Brumbaugh, Susan, 18, 23, 50
Champion, Dean J., 13, 19-20, 24-25, 29
Chau, Michelle, 10
Chesney-Lind, Meda, 9-11, 18, 20, 29, 31, 49, 52
Chia, Louise, 42
Children, female responsibilities, 150
Classification, 24
   Walnut Street jail, 24

Clear, Todd R., 26, 61
Clements, Carl B., 19, 26
Comack, Elizabeth, 10-11, 61, 165
Community corrections,
    Growth in population, 13, 18
Context, importance of, 51
    in risk/need instruments, 161-169
        objectivity, 157
        victimization, impact of, 157, 165-169
Coulson, Grant, 36, 39, 109
Couture, Heather, 4
Correctional industrial complex, 18
Covington, Stephanie, 4, 6-7, 9-12, 29-31, 37, 41, 43-44, 52, 61, 71, 161, 165
Criminogenic needs, 26
Crow, Jason, 27-28, 56, 161
Crowley, Michael, 19, 33-34, 45
Cudjoe, Francis, 36, 39, 109
Cullen, Francis T., 13, 22-23, 25-26, 32-33, 36-38, 40, 45, 50, 80, 110
Cupp, Rhonda, 4, 13, 15, 23-24, 29-33, 35-38, 41, 47, 51-54, 56-57, 162, 164
Daly, Kathleen, 11, 29, 49
DeMatteo, David, 30-31, 40
Desautels, Amy, 4-6
Deschenes, Elizabeth P., 27-28, 56, 162
Ditton, Paula M., 10, 143
Domains, qualitative analysis. *See also*, LSI-R,
        accommodations, 129-131
        cost of living, 129-130
        alcohol & drugs, 134-138
        context, 135-138
        victimization, 136-138
    attitudes & orientation, 142-143
    companions, 133-134
    criminal histories,
        male/female comparisons, 115-119
    education & employment, 119-121
    emotional & personal, 139-142
        mental health, 139-142
        treatment, 140-142
        victimization, 139-142
    family & marital relationships, 125-129
        protective versus risk, 126
        troubled relationships, 126-129
        victimization, 125-129
    financial status, 122-124
    leisure & recreation, 131-133
Douglas, Kevin S., 37, 40-41, 43, 50, 56-57, 76, 80
Dowden, Craig, 14, 45
Duclos, Christian Wilson, 62
Dynamic factors, 26
Epistemology, 3, 6
Erickson, Jacey, 30-31, 40
Fagan, Abigail, 27, 37, 57
Fagan, Jeffrey, 4, 7, 49, 66, 73
Farr, Kathryn, Ann, 10, 29, 36-37, 41
Farrington, David P., 25, 29, 37
Feely, Malcolm, 22, 23, 27

Index

Female offenders
    context of offending, 1-2, 7, 9
    criminal justice growth, 12
    differences from males, 9
    dysfunctional relationships, 11
    invisibility, 5
    mental health issues, 10
    neglect in research &theory, 1, 3-7, 14
    patterns of offending, 4
    risk, 3, 61
    victimization, 10-11, 31, 54
Female only samples, 53
Feminization of poverty, 159
Flavin, Jeanne, 4-6, 41
Flowers, R. Barri, 8
Foucault, Michael, 21
Fretz, Ralph, 30-31, 40
Funk, Stephanie J., 14, 34-35, 37-38, 54, 56, 62
Gartner, Rosemary, 10, 18, 41
Gelsthorpe, Loraine, 7
Gender,
    as predictive of criminal offending, 4
    as variable, problems with 53
    neutrality in risk assessments, 157
    roles, 5
    sex versus gender, 5-6
Gender-specific needs, 30
Gilfus, Mary E., 7, 10-11, 60, 61-62, 66, 68, 81, 111, 115, 152, 160, 166, 171
Giulekas, Diana, 36, 39, 109
Glaze, Lauren E., 4, 12, 18
Goertzel, Ted, 59, 161
Gottfredson, Don M., 20, 23-27, 43, 46-47, 170, 175
Gottfredson, Stephen, D., 23-28, 36, 170, 176
Hagedorn, John M., 8
Hamilton, Zachary, 37-38, 54
Hannah-Moffat, Kelly, 4, 7, 14, 23, 26-30, 34-37, 41-42, 44, 46-47, 49, 54-55, 57, 60-61, 70, 155, 161-162, 176
Harcourt, Bernard E., 13-14, 19-20, 22, 24-25, 32, 43, 47, 163, 171, 173-174, 176
Harer, Miles D., 14, 38
Harlow, Caroline Wolf, 30
Hawkins, David J., 27, 37, 57
Health, male and female problems, 150
Heilbrun, Kirk, 30-31, 40
Hiller-Sturmhofel, Susanne, 166, 168
Hirschi, Travis, 168
Hoge, R.D., 26, 74
Hollin, Clive R., 10-11, 14, 23, 27, 29-30, 34, 36, 47, 110, 116, 119, 134, 139, 142-143, 161, 164 166, 170
Holsinger, Alexander M., 14, 17, 19, 23-25, 38-39, 43, 109

Holsinger, Kristi, 4
Holtfreter, Kristy, 4, 7, 10, 13-15, 23-24, 27, 29-41, 47, 51-54, 56-57, 64, 66, 111, 125, 162-165, 170, 175, 176
Hubbard, Dana Jones 14, 29-30, 34-35, 37, 39, 41, 44, 56-57
Hudson, Barbara, 13, 171-173
Ilacqua, Giorgio, 36, 39, 109
Interviews, qualitative, 68, 71, 115
    analysis of, thematic coding, 68
    guides, 68, 70
    informed consent, 67
    length of, 68
    location of, 66
    recording of, 67
James, Dorris J., 41-42, 143-144
Jamieson, Janet, 4, 7, 29
Jones, Dana A., 13, 26
Jones, Peter R., 19, 70
Jones, Stephen, 8
Kiessling, Jerry J., 45
Kruttschnitt, Candace, 10, 18, 41
Langan, Patrick A., 56, 84
Latessa, Edward J., 14, 17, 19, 22-26, 32-33, 35-40, 42-43, 45, 50, 80, 109, 110
Laub, John H., 7
Lawrence, Sharmila, 10
Lennon, Mary Clare, 10
Levin, David J., 56, 84
Level of Service Inventory-Revised (LSI-R), 15, 32, 50, 52-53, 55-56, 59, 62, 73-74, 113
    alcohol & drug, 2
    content validity, 1-2, 47, 125, 156, 160, 175
    correlations with outcome, 80-84, 85-93
    criminogenic risks and needs, 32, 42
    cut off scores, females, 42
    domains, 32, 34, 115-142,
    domain differences, gender, 1, 76-79, 80-81
    efficacy for females, 160-161, 175
    female offender issues, 34
    future directions, 169-171
    gender, problems related to 36
    gender comparisons, 74
    kaplan-meier analysis, 94-106
    lack of context, females, 42, 114, 151-154
    lack of gender-neutrality, 15, 33-35, 43
    lack of objectivity, 43
    male-based research, 15, 33
    over-classification and gender, 41-42, 106-108, 170
    predictive validity, 1-2, 157-159, 175
    purpose, 32-33
    research,
    risk levels, with outcome, 85
    scoring, 32
    social learning theory, 32
    survival analysis, 84
    survival strategies, 159
    theory, lack of gender, 62

Index

treatment, 33
under-classification, 41-42, 106-108, 170
use in Hawai'i, 45
Loader, Ian, 14, 19, 23, 27, 45
Lowenkamp, Christopher L., 17, 19, 38, 50, 109
LSI-R, Research. *See also*, Level of Service Inventory-Revised
   abuse, effect of, 39
   gender comparisons, 74
   gendered pathways, 114
   gender-specific, 37, 39, 40
      lack of, female offender, 37, 38, 43-44, 50, 53
   gender-specific factors, effect of, 40-41
   male-based validation, 36-37
   mixed gender, 38-39
   reliability, 36-37
   risk levels, with outcome, 85
   survival analysis, 84
   validation, 36, 38-39, 56
Lurigio, Author J., 4, 7, 14, 19, 23-25, 34-37, 39, 41, 43, 57, 109
Lynch, Mary, 46
Manchak, Sarah M., 37, 40-41, 43, 50, 56-57, 76, 80
Masculinities research, 7-8
Mass incarceration, 18
Matthews, Betsy, 29-30, 34-35, 41, 44, 56-57
Mauer, Marc, 18
Maurutto, Paula, 7, 27-28, 37, 44, 47, 161
Maxfield, Michael G., 144

McDiarmid, Anne, 9, 168
McLvor, Gill, 4, 7, 29
McMahon, Maeve, 43
Messerschmidt, James W., 8
Mickus, Susan, 45
Miller, Jody, 8
Miller, Susan L., 49, 51, 55, 67-68, 167-168
Minton, Todd D., 4
Mixed gender models, 54
Modley, Phyllis, 11
Morash, Merry, 5, 7, 10, 12, 14, 27, 30, 34-35, 39-41, 51, 54, 64, 66, 111, 163-165, 170, 175-176
Motiuk, Laurence L., 19, 33-34, 45, 56
Mumola, Christopher J., 82
Murray, Cathy, 4, 7, 29
New penology, 22-23. *See also*, Risk Management
Nutbrown, Verna, 36, 39, 109
Olson, David E., 4, 7, 14, 34-37, 39, 41, 57, 109
Owen, Barbara, 4, 9-12, 27-31, 34, 41, 43, 47, 52, 56, 60- 61, 70-71, 161-162, 165
Painter, Kate A. 27, 29
Palmer, Emma J., 10-11, 14, 23, 27, 29-30, 34, 36, 47, 110, 116, 119, 134, 139, 142-143, 161, 164, 166, 170
Pang, Bessie, 42
Parsons, Mickey L., 10
Pasko, Lisa, 11, 20

Pathways perspective,
  offending as survival strategy, 10-11
  research implications, 61
  role of victimization, 10-11
  substance use, 10
  theoretical framework, 9, 12
  to criminal offending, 9
Patriarchy, 11
Pelz, Beth,
Petersilia, Joan, 18, 26, 36, 62, 169-170
Pratt, Travis C., 14, 37, 39
Presser, Lois, 34, 35, 42
Price, Ronald, 17
Prisoners,
  female inmate grown, 12
  growth in population, 12, 18
Protective factors, 114, 162
Proxy, screen, 74
Raynor, Peter, 30, 40
Recidivism, rates of, 75
Research,
  content validity, importance of, 60
  cox regression, 59, 84
  female only samples, 53
  feminist methods, 50
  feminist standpoint, need for, 6, 50-51
  gender as variable, problems with, 53
  generalizability of male-based findings, 7, 49, 52
  lack of feminist standpoint, 6
  measurement, 52
  mixed gender models, 54
  multiple methods, use of 51, 55
  separate gender models, benefit of 54
  survival analysis, 59, 84
  qualitative methods, utility of 51, 60-61
  quantitative methods, problems with, 51
Reisig, Michael D., 7, 10, 14, 27, 30, 34, 39-41, 54, 64, 66, 111, 163, 165, 170, 175-176
Richards, Stephen C., 62
Richie, Beth E., 11, 34, 71, 167
Risk management, 17, 19, 22
  See also New penology
Risk/need assessment instrument.
  See also actuarial instruments, LSI-R.
  contemporary use of, 13
  content validity, 55
  context, lack of 113
  ethical issues, 171-176
  false negatives / positives, 24
  gender-neutrality, lack of, 13-14, 27-32, 50, 56
  generalizability, 52
  management of correctional populations, 14
  need for gendered instruments, 162, 170-171, 175-176
  new penology, 27
  over-classification, 31
  predictive ability, 26-27
  rehabilitation, 23, 28
  research, 53
  spurious relationships, 114
  third-generation,, 23, 27-28

Index

treatment, 23, 28
under-classification, 31
validity, 31
Risk principle, 23, 74
Robinson, David 45
Sabol, William J., 4, 12-13, 18
Salisbury, Emily, 4, 9-10, 14, 26-27, 29-31, 36-37, 40-41, 82, 162
Sample description,
    qualitative, 69
        incentives, 64-65
        recruitment of, 63-64, 65
    quantitative, 58
Sampson, Robert J., 7
Separate gender models, benefit of, 54
Severson, Margaret, 62
Shaw, Margaret, 23, 26, 28, 29-30, 34-35, 41-42, 46, 57, 60-61, 70, 176
Simon, Jonathan, 22, 23, 27, 119
Siranosian, Maro, 37, 40-41, 43, 50, 56-57, 76, 80
Skeem, Jenifer L., 37, 40-41, 43, 50, 56-57, 76, 80
Smith, David J., 9
Smith, Paula, 13, 22-23, 25-26, 32-33, 36-38, 40, 45, 50, 80, 110
Snell, Tracy L., 4
Social assistance, 119-124
    context, 122, 123
    context of drug treatment, 119-121
    females, 119-121
    risk versus protective factors, 122-124
Sparks, Richard, 14, 19, 23, 27, 45
Snyder, Howard N., 23, 43, 46-47
Sommers, Ira, 4, 7, 49, 66, 73
Sprague, Joey, 5-6, 50-51, 53-55, 60, 65, 161, 163-164, 166, 168
Static factors, 26
Steffey, Danielle M., 18, 23, 50
Stuart, Bryan, 13, 29
Tarling, Roger, 25, 37
Taylor, Kelly N., 50, 47, 55, 57, 162
Tonry, Michael, 18, 171, 174
Validity
    content, 55
    predictive, 1
Van Horn, M.L., 27, 37, 57
Van Voorhis, Patricia, 4, 9, 10, 14, 23, 25-27, 29-31, 33-37, 40-42, 45, 60, 82, 107, 162, 171
Veysey, Bonita M., 37, 38, 54
Victimization, *See also* female offenders.
    description of, 143-149
    female offenders, 10
    Impact on offending
    left out of LSI-R, 143, 149
    link with alcohol and drug use, 144, 148
    male and female differences, 143-144
    scope of, 143-149
    survival strategies, 10-11
    trajectories, 10-11

Vose, Brenda, 13, 32, 36, 38
Wallance-Carpetta, Suzanne, 42
Warner-Robbins, Carmen, 10
Warren, Jennifer, 18
West, Heather C., 12, 13, 18
Whitaker, Mary Scully, 34, 41
Widom, Cathy S., 10, 30, 144, 166, 168
Wright, Jen, 33
Wright, Emily, 4, 9, 10, 14, 26-27, 29-31, 36-37, 40-41, 82, 162
Yasuhara, Kento, 30-31, 40
Zamble, Edward, 25, 27